As one of th...
a...
Thomas Cook are the experts in travel.

For more than 135 years our
guidebooks have unlocked the secrets
of destinations around the world,
sharing with travellers a wealth of
experience and a passion for travel.

**Rely on Thomas Cook as your
travelling companion on your next trip
and benefit from our unique heritage.**

...uides

LO... ...Y
Kathy Arnold & Paul Wade

Thomas Cook

Your travelling companion since 1873

Written by Kathy Arnold and Paul Wade, updated by Alex Stewart
Original photography by Bob Moore

Published by Thomas Cook Publishing
A division of Thomas Cook Tour Operations Limited
Company registration no. 3772199 England
The Thomas Cook Business Park, Unit 9, Coningsby Road,
Peterborough PE3 8SB, United Kingdom
Email: books@thomascook.com, Tel: +44 (0) 1733 416477
www.thomascookpublishing.com

Produced by Cambridge Publishing Management Limited
Burr Elm Court, Main Street, Caldecote CB23 7NU

ISBN: 978-1-84848-476-4

© 2004 Thomas Cook Publishing
This second edition © 2011
Text © Thomas Cook Publishing
Maps © Thomas Cook Publishing/PCGraphics (UK) Limited

Series Editor: Karen Beaulah
Production/DTP: Steven Collins

Printed and bound in Spain by GraphyCems

Cover photography © Steve Vidler/SuperStock

Contents

Introduction

The Loire Valley in central France is considered to be the Garden of France and the home of the French language. Celebrated for its past, its historic towns and its architectural heritage, it inspires romantic visions of splendid, fairytale châteaux and cultural monuments. The region has been sculpted by the centuries of interaction between people and the physical environment, particularly the Loire River, to produce a unique landscape, a large stretch of which is recognised by UNESCO as a World Heritage Site.

Behind this fantastic front, however, is a region with a reputation for gentleness and sophistication. Further from Paris than its geographic distance suggests, this quiet corner harks back to an older age when it was the playground of kings and their courts. Azay-le-Rideau, Chambord, Chenonceau, Cheverny and Ussé compete with Valençay and Villandry for your attention. Amboise, Beaugency, Blois, Chinon and Loches also clamour to be seen. Larger towns such as Orléans and Tours combine history and contemporary culture to stunning effect.

Whatever you choose to see, though, don't forget to enjoy the region for the same reasons that made the French royalty first come here: soft light, a favourable climate, a gentle landscape and countryside full of charm and character. The Loire and its impressive tributaries idle past, giving rise to the region's fertility. Fantastic local produce and internationally celebrated wines are available in even the smallest village. Drive the back roads, walk the riverbanks or cycle the quiet lanes to come away with a far better and broader appreciation of this beautiful, cultured part of France.

High and mighty: Saumur's castle has dominated the landscape for five centuries

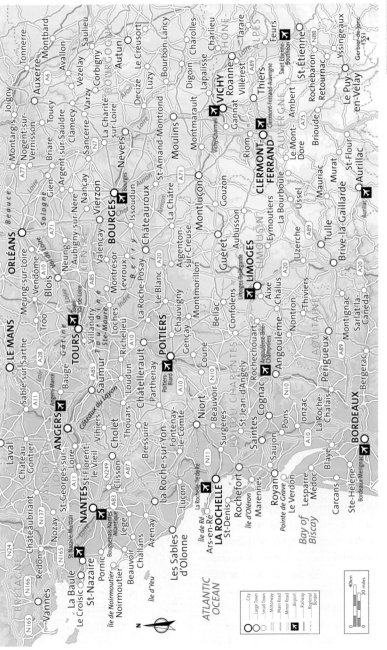

The land

If there is one physical feature that unites the 450km (280 miles) of the valley of the Loire, from Nantes to Nevers, it has to be overall flatness. There are no granite outcrops or towering escarpments, no ranges of high hills or cavernous gorges. There are, however, gentle undulations where the Loire and its side rivers have cut through the ubiquitous limestone to produce cliffs, often topped by a castle.

A well-lit landscape

Sweeping horizons and vast skyscapes flood the region with light: châteaux are silhouetted against blue skies, vineyards and wheatfields are drenched with sunshine and even small clumps of trees look prettier in the region's clear light. North and south of Angers, away from the Loire, are patchworks of small, hedged fields and farms; the slopes running down to the river itself are covered in vines. East of Angers, where the River Authion runs almost parallel to the Loire, the fertile soil is worked by market gardeners and nurserymen.

Limestone and forest

The region's chalky white rock has been quarried for centuries to build palaces and mansions, castles and abbeys. The resulting holes in the cliffs have been used as homes (*caves troglodites*) by ordinary folk. The once-abundant forests have been chopped down to build the scores of medieval houses that still survive in almost all the region's towns and cities. On the southern side of the Loire, around Saumur, low cliffs of *tuffe* (tufa) are riddled with ancient caves and tunnels, now recycled for use as wine storage cellars and mushroom farms.

Fertile fields

Further south in the Saumur region are vines. In the north around Baugé, the ancient forest has now dwindled to scattered areas of woodland, interspersed with fields of sunflowers and maize. Between Saumur and Tours, the broad valley is filled with orchards and vegetable growers. To the south is Sainte-Maure, the plateau which gives its name to the famous goat's cheese. North of Tours is the Gâtine; now drained and cultivated, the area consists of a mixture of fields, woodland and open heath.

Forests, marshes and vines

South of Orléans is the region known as the Sologne where the thick forests near

Orléans are slowly being invaded by golf courses. This traditional land of misty, murky marshes has also been changed by the extraction of clay for brick making, leaving behind a series of ponds. Now rather scrubby, this is the flattest part of the region, covered in small pines and heather and still known for its hunting.

North of Orléans are the plains of the Beauce, with its endless fields of wheat and for centuries the breadbasket of France. Finally, to the south of Gien, the corrugated slopes along the Loire are embroidered with vines; these grow the Sauvignon Blanc grapes that produce the famous Sancerre and Pouilly wines.

Regions and economy

The great expanse of the Loire Valley encompasses several age-old provinces that were once important names in French history: Orléanais, the largest; Touraine, known for its wealth; and Anjou, the land of the Plantagenets. Now this area is divided between the Pays de la Loire and the Centre-Val-de-Loire. Both are modern bureaucratic inventions that embrace half-a-dozen *départements*.

The Pays de la Loire

Enveloping the western end of the Loire Valley, the Pays de la Loire has some three million inhabitants scattered over 32,500sq km (12,548sq miles). Nantes, the administrative capital, and Angers together account for some 820,000 of the population, the rest being spread around the towns and villages of the wide-open countryside. About one in ten is employed in agriculture, where there has been a dramatic drop in

Hidden treasure: Montsoreau's wine is stored deep in the cliffs

Don't get confused: Le Loir is a pretty tributary of the bigger Loire

employment in the last two decades, emphasising a rise in efficiency rarely recognised outside France. This is one of France's principal livestock rearing regions, but the processing of fresh produce is just as important. Canning companies, such as Fleury Michon and Saupiquet, dairies such as the group Lactalis, and biscuit and cake manufacturers, such as BN and LU, all make a substantial contribution to the local economy. In Angers, the humble orange is transformed into Cointreau liqueur.

Nantes is France's third most important city financially while the thriving leather and shoe industry has long been a Vendée speciality.

Centre-Val-de-Loire

This area, combining Touraine and Berry, with Orléans as the administrative capital, includes large tracts of forest and the semi-wilderness of the Sologne. It is even more sparsely populated than the Pays de la Loire, with fewer than 2.5 million inhabitants, spread over 40,000sq km (15,444sq miles), an average of 62.5 people per sq km. Here, too, farming claims 10 per cent of the workforce in an area that ranks as the fourth biggest in agricultural production in France, while in the region north of Orléans, the Beauce ranks number one for cereals. Significant local employers include the automotive industry: Matra cars at Romorantin, SNIAS at Bourges and Michelin at Joué-les-Tours. Overall, 16,000 people are employed in the car industry, with Renault being the most important employer. The electronic and computer industry is the third-largest employer and includes Thomson, Alcatel and

Sagem. The region's combined electronic, chemical and pharmaceutical production ranks second only to Île-de-France in the whole country and it is often referred to as Cosmetic Valley.

Tourism

Tourism is important to the Loire Valley economy, but the people here have recognised that being the land of famous châteaux is not enough. In every city and town, scaffolding signifies that work is in progress to restore medieval and Renaissance buildings. Great effort is put into

TRIBUTARIES OF THE LOIRE

The Loire is famous for its noble châteaux, though many of the finest are not on the Loire itself; tributaries such as the Cher, Indre, Vienne and Layon (flowing into the Loire from the south), and the Cisse, Loir, Sarthe, Mayenne and Oudon (entering from the north) all have their own attractive châteaux set in landscapes of great variety.

The land

maintaining traditional cultural events and regional festivals.

The quality of life in the Loire Valley has been celebrated for centuries; locals are working hard to keep it that way.

Limestone gives Saumur its nickname of La Ville Blanche (the white town)

The Loire

The Loire is the longest river in France. It bubbles up at Gerbier-de-Jonc only 150km (93 miles) from the Mediterranean. It then flows north for much of its course, before sweeping westwards at Sancerre towards the Atlantic. The statistics are impressive: the Loire is over 1,000km (621 miles) long, with a 1,400m (1-mile) drop in altitude from the source high in the Cévennes mountains to the 3km- (2-mile) wide mouth at St-Nazaire on the Atlantic coast. On the way, the river cuts through 11 *départements* and drains water from one-fifth of the whole land area of France.

For centuries the Loire was a major transport route, carrying goods and people. Timber, fruit and wine would be loaded aboard flat-bottomed *chalands* and *gabarres*, boats that could slide on and off the notorious shoals and sandbanks without damage. Fish from the Atlantic would be kept alive in tanks of salt water and rowed slowly upstream against the current. Only in the 19th century did the coming of the railway diminish its importance.

Today, roads follow built-up embankments, often looking down to the river on one side and to the roofs of houses on the other. Broad and flat, the Loire may appear docile, but it is a dangerous river. Some *turcies* (earthen ramparts) were built 1,000 years ago in an early attempt to control the floods. Further defences

A deceptive tranquillity

Sandbanks abound, even in the heart of Orléans

were built along the Authion tributary in the 12th century; *levées* (raised banks) were built by Colbert, the finance minister of King Louis XIV, in the 17th century. Still the floods ripped through, causing disasters in 1846, 1856 and 1866. Even now the Loire bursts its banks, and floods the surrounding countryside. Major plans are afoot to spend a considerable sum to prevent this problem.

Flooding is not the only danger. Between the river's islands are the treacherous *sables mouvants* (quicksands) ready to suck in the unwary picnicker or walker. *Tourbillons* (whirlpools) do the same to kayaks and canoes exploring the apparently innocuous *boires* (side channels) or *luisettes* (rivulets).

Modern developments have also made their mark. Atomic power stations occasionally scar the landscape and, since 1989, the TGV high-speed train has brought Paris within commuting distance.

Despite this, nature remains in charge of the Loire. Stately herons and flickering kingfishers, catfish and *sandre* (zander) all abound, and even the salmon are making an enthusiastic come-back. Everywhere the land seems fertile. No wonder it attracted the nobility of France and was called the Vallée des Rois – the Valley of the Kings.

History

52 BC–5th century AD
The Loire Valley comes within the Roman province of Lugdunensis.

AD 250
St Gatien is sent from Rome to convert Gaul to Christianity, becoming the first bishop of Tours.

451
The Huns leave Gaul.

732
Charles Martel defeats the Moors (Saracens) at Poitiers.

11th century
The region's first major stone fortifications are constructed by Foulques III Nerra (*see p68*), the ambitious Comte d'Anjou.

1154
Henri Plantagenet, Comte d'Anjou, is crowned King Henry II of England.

1189
The death of Henry II, at Chinon, marks the start of a 300-year struggle between the kings of England and France for supremacy in the Loire Valley.

1337
The Hundred Years War begins as King Edward III of England pushes his claim to French territory.

1417
King Henry V of England is recognised by the Treaty of Troyes as heir to the throne of France.

1429
Jeanne d'Arc (Joan of Arc) defeats the English at Orléans.

1460–1600
The flowering of the 'Royal Valley of the Loire'. Successive kings build châteaux and courtly life flourishes.

1519
Great artists and writers flourish in the region. Leonardo da Vinci dies at Amboise.

1562–98
The Wars of Religion (*see p57*).

1789
The French Revolution begins, followed four years later by the Vendée Wars in which royalists revolt against the republicans.

1832
The first steamboat chugs down the River Loire, but the railways soon take over, marking the river's decline as a transport link.

1870	The Prussians capture Châteaudun, Orléans, Tours and Azay-le-Rideau during the month-long Franco-Prussian War.
1940	During World War II, France's aged Marshal Pétain shakes hands with Hitler at Montoire-sur-le-Loire, a symbol of collaboration with the enemy. The River Cher divides Occupied and 'Vichy' France.
1969	France's first and controversial atomic power station opens at Avoine, near Chinon, on the Loire.
1989	The TGV high-speed train links the Loire Valley to Paris.
2000	Inauguration of the 'Pont de l'Europe', the 100th bridge to span the Loire. The Loire Valley is made one of UNESCO's World Heritage Sites.
2005	Government grants and a change in law regarding restoration encourage château owners to work on their properties. A state of emergency is declared after civil unrest sweeps France's urban areas.
2006	The Loire à Vélo cycle route from Orléans downstream to Aneers is officially opened.
2007	Nicolas Sarkozy sweeps to power against a backdrop of discontent regarding issues of unemployment, immigration and healthcare, securing a higher than average amount of support in the Loire region.
2008	A smoking ban in public places becomes law. France's 35-hour working week is scrapped as employers are allowed to enforce a longer week on staff.
2010	Unemployment in France hits 10%. The government attempts to enforce an increase in retirement age from 60 to 62. Sarkozy suffers a series of bruising defeats in regional elections as strikes and massive disruption once again cripple France, leaving him an enormous challenge to unite the country and move forward.

Politics

Politically, the Loire Valley is a conservative area. Tours, for example, had a right-wing mayor for 35 years who, although popular for his conservation projects, was nevertheless criticised for the lack of investment in industry. In local elections, voters support the individual, not a party. Communist mayors are not uncommon, and Orléans, traditionally right-wing, moved left in the 1990s but at the last elections voted in a far right-wing mayor from the RPR party. French politics is unpredictable.

Political parties

France has five recognisable political parties. The UMP (Union for a Popular Movement), headed by President Sarkozy and Prime Minister Fillon, is a major player and an heir to the old Gaullist RPR (Rally for the Republic) Party. It encourages privatisation, low taxes and business. The old right-of-centre Union for French Democracy (UDF) disintegrated in 2007 to be replaced by the pro-UMP Nouveau Centre (NC) Party. The PS (Socialist Party) has moved towards the centre (pro-Europe and pro-NATO) while the PCF (French Communist Party) has slumped in popularity since World War II. The FN (National Front), the ultra-right-wing party led by Jean-Marie le Pen received a lot of publicity but remains a minor outfit.

Administration

Justice, education and health remain national responsibilities. In the next layer down, France is divided into 22 regions, of which the Pays de la Loire (Western Loire) and Centre-Val-de-Loire are two. The regions administer tourism, cultural heritage, industrial development and adult education. Below the regional level are France's 96 *départements*, which oversee social services and welfare. Finally, the *départements* are further subdivided into 36,500 *communes*, each headed by a mayor who is often a powerful political figure, responsible for local planning, building and environmental controls.

National politics

Nicolas Sarkozy was elected president in a closely contested election in 2007, ushering in an era of personality-led politics previously not seen in France. The conservative François Fillon, from Le Mans in the Pays de la Loire region, was appointed prime minister. Sarkozy defeated his Socialist rival by ostensibly promising to undertake a series of radical reforms. The result was divisive and by the end of the year civil servants and other workers were protesting on the streets.

In 2008 a wave of general strikes was accompanied by rioting in Paris. Following his whirlwind relationship and wedding to former model and musician Carla Bruni, Sarkozy's ratings went into freefall as he was accused of arrogance, vanity and trying to control the media. Local elections in 2008 saw the Socialists recapture a number of seats. Today, the Socialist Party control many of the urban areas of Pays de la Loire including Angers, Le Mans, Nantes and Tours. Despite further heavy defeats in the regional elections in 2010, it is likely that Sarkozy will contest the next election in 2012, in a bid to secure a second term.

Politics

A former hotbed of political conspiracy: Château d'Amboise

Festivals and events

The Loire has a tradition of hosting festivals and major events. In keeping with its location, landscape and customs, many of these are musical or themed around regional produce. Locals throng at these occasions but visitors are just as welcome and it is a superb way of rubbing shoulders with people from the region. For a list of fairs in the Loire Valley, please see p183.

January
La Folle Journé Hundreds of classical concerts over five days in Nantes. *www.follejournee.fr*

February
Chalonnes-sur-Loire Celebration of the wines of Saumur and Anjou with tastings, seminars and walks through the vineyards during the last weekend in February.

March
Les Printemps Musical de St-Cosme Chamber music festival promoting young musicians in the Priory of St-Cosme in Tours.

April
Les Printemps de Bourges Rock music festival with massive attendance in Bourges. *www.printemps-bourges.com*
Festival International des Jardins Landscape garden festival at Château Chaumont that runs until mid-October. *www.domaine-chaumont.fr*

Fêtes de Jeanne d'Arc Medieval festival and market, concerts and exhibitions at the end of April and early May in Orléans celebrating the city's liberation by the eponymous heroine. *www.fetesjeannedarc.com*
Cadre Noir Outstanding horse-riding demonstration shows from April to October in Saumur. *www.cadrenoir.fr*

June
Festival d'Anjou Second largest theatre festival in France, in Angers. *www.festivaldanjou.com*
Game Fair National hunting and fishing festival in the third week of the month in Chambord. *www.gamefair.fr*
Jazz Festival Free concerts throughout Chinon.
Le Printemps des Arts de Nantes Baroque music festival. *www.printempsdesarts.fr*
Fêtes Musical en Touraine Prestigious chamber music festival in Tours.
Rendez-vous aux jardins Famous and less well-known gardens, including

many in the Loire region, are opened to the public.
www.rendezvousauxjardins.culture.fr

July

Classical music festival Runs from mid-July to mid-Aug in Amboise.

Franco-Scottish Festival Celebration of the Auld Alliance (*see pp121, 124*) on the weekend closest to Bastille Day (July 14) in Aubigny-sur-Nère.

Tous sur le Pont Five-day music festival held in the courtyard of the château in Blois. *www.toussurlepont.com*

Les Heures Musicales Festival of organ chamber music in the abbey in Cunault and nearby church at Trèves.
http://amisndcunault.free.fr

Journées de la Rose Very big rose and flower festival lasting a week in Doué-la-Fontaine. *www.journeesdelarose.com*

Concours Complet International Major horse-riding competition in Saumur.

Gastronomic festival At the end of the month, featuring cookery and market stalls selling food in Tours.

Nuits des Mille Feux Two nights in early July when the gardens at Villandry are illuminated by two thousand candles, while actors and acrobats entertain the crowds before a giant firework display.
www.chateauvillandry.com

August

Festival International de Folklore One of France's largest folk music festivals in Montoire-sur-le-Loire.
www.festival-montoire.com

Les Rendez-vous de l'Erdre Jazz festival in Nantes, with a nautical theme, during the last week of the month and with more than 45 free concerts.
www.rendezvouserdre.com

Les Grandes Tablées du Saumur Champigny Vast gastronomic festival over two days centred on regional food and Champigny wine and held in Saumur.

Musique et jardins Classical concerts in the château gardens at Villandry.

September

Festival Européen de Musique Renaissance Three-day music festival at Clos Lucé. *www.vinci-closluce.com*

Festival de Loire Five-day music and entertainment spectacle at the end of the month with hundreds of boats moored on the quays at Orléans.
www.festivaldeloire.com

October

Le Lion d'Angers International horse show focusing on dressage and cross-country.
www.mondialdulion.com

Les Rockomotives Large pop and rock music festival in Vendôme.
www.rockomotives.com

November

Euro Gusto Food festival that takes place every two years, on odd numbered years, with wide range of wines and regional foods to sample, workshops to join and demonstrations to watch.
www.eurogusto.org

Impressions

The people of the Loire are totally French in outlook and manners, and they have no distinctive character traits or looks. Neither do they have a peasant folklore, colourful costumes, music or dances. What they have long had, however, according to 19th-century novelist Honoré de Balzac, is 'a refined spirit, a politeness that befits a region that the kings of France have taken to their hearts'.

Even today, the inhabitants of the Loire are still 'completely relaxed, because they have so little character', according to contemporary novelist Jean-Marie Laclavetine. His view, that this welcoming, relaxed attitude is due to a lack of character, is not a criticism; rather he is complimenting people for their moderation and lack of confrontation.

Great architecture and good wine

Their equable nature reflects the environment, which has neither extremes of climate nor of landscape. The ingredients of the good life are readily to hand, from field, stream and vineyard. No wonder locals boast of their *art de bien vivre*, an 'art of living well' that includes not just a love of fine food and wine but also a developed culture that dates back to the French Renaissance, which, after all, had its origins in the Loire 500 years ago. All this is good news for international visitors. From hoteliers to campsite managers and from guides to wine-growers, everyone is used to dealing with tourists and understands the different tastes of different nationalities.

There is a welcome informality throughout the region, so 'smart-casual' clothing is acceptable almost everywhere, except in churches and cathedrals where shorts and sleeveless tops are seen as offensive. The custom of muttering '*M'sieurs, dames*' on entering a shop or restaurant prevails, as does the handshake with new acquaintances.

With English now the region's second language, it is easy to strike up conversations – but do take advice with a pinch of salt. The local wine and the local château will always be recommended because, despite their worldliness, the people of the Loire believe that their home town or village is the best place on earth.

Getting about

The Loire Valley has a mixture of main roads for fast intercity traffic and delightfully rural lanes for gentle sightseeing. Motorways link Le Mans to Angers and Nantes, while Orléans is connected to Tours and Bourges. Although the main riverside roads can be very busy – sometimes limited to only one lane in each direction on a high dike or embankment – there is usually a quiet, if meandering, riverside road on the opposite bank of the Loire. Since the countryside is generally flat or gently undulating, this is especially good cycling country, and a large-scale map makes it easy for cyclists to follow the well-paved minor roads.

The architecture

Chenonceau and Azay-le-Rideau, mirrored in water; Ussé, with its fairy-tale towers; Chambord, the grandiose royal hunting lodge; and Cheverny, the country mansion – these are the architectural descendants of the simple wood and earth forts of northern

Royal presence: King Louis XII was born and held court in Blois

France, originally built in the 8th and 9th centuries as protection against quarrelsome neighbours as well as Viking and Muslim raiders. Their evolution can be traced over 800 years.

8th–11th centuries

First came the motte-and-bailey construction. The motte was an earthen mound defended by a deep ditch. At the base of the mound, the 'bailey' was a stockade enclosing farm buildings and storehouses. On top of the mound, another stockade defended a fort, as in the reconstruction in the Parc de la

Haie-Joulain at Saint-Sylvain d'Anjou near Angers. Timber forts were later rebuilt in stone, resulting in the *donjon* (a keep, not a dungeon). Foulques III Nerra (*see p68*) built many such *donjons*, the remains of which can be seen at Langeais (*see p66*), Loches (*see pp67–8*) and Beaugency (*see p91*).

12th–13th centuries

Military architects, learning from the lessons of the Crusades, built curtain walls to protect the buildings of the inner keep, with circular lookout towers at intervals around the walls. Narrow slits allowed archers to fire outwards, and machicolations (holes in the floor) were used for dropping stones and quicklime, but not boiling oil, on attackers. At Angers (*see p24*) and Chinon (*see p62*), the impressive walls, their smoothness an added protection, encompassed extensive living quarters and chapels.

14th–15th centuries

Once the Hundred Years War with England was over in 1453, defence gave way to grandeur, and feudal castles (originally built as purposeful structures) evolved into homes and pleasure palaces. With the siege a thing of the past, châteaux became less a place to hide and more a means of signifying status and wealth, with new comfort and intricate design the priorities. At Langeais (*see p66*), built between 1465 and 1469, turreted towers are softened by domestic-looking gables

and larger windows. Older castles were remodelled and given fine interiors. Moats became mirrors and water gardens rather than defences. By the late 15th century, several châteaux were being renovated as royal palaces. At Amboise (*see p58*), King Charles VIII surrounded himself with luxurious furnishings copied from the grand palaces of Italy.

16th century

King Louis XII (reigned 1498–1515) established his court at Blois (*see pp91–2*). His successor King François I enlarged Amboise and built Chambord (*see pp92–3*), while his Secretary of State created Villandry (*see p77*) with its magnificent gardens. Chenonceau (*see pp60–61*) was made grand first by the mistress of King Henri II, Diane de Poitiers, and then by his widow, Catherine de'Medici. The end of the royal era in the Loire came in 1598 when King Henri IV, the first of the Bourbons, moved the court back to Paris.

17th–18th centuries

Even without the king, the Loire continued to attract the wealthy and the aristocratic. Cheverny was built (*see pp98–9*), and at Saumur (*see p46*) and Chaumont (*see p60*) walls were removed to open up the vistas. Violence returned, however, when many châteaux were stripped bare or destroyed during the French Revolution (1789–92).

Saumur's medieval fortress overlooking the Loire

The Western Loire

The city of Nantes (once the capital of Brittany) sits at the westernmost end of the Val de Loire. To the east is Saumur, known as 'la ville blanche' (the white town) because of the soft white tufa limestone quarried nearby. In between these two is Angers, historic capital of the Counts of Anjou, known as 'la ville noire' (the black town) because of its nearby slate mines. The centuries-old rivalry dates back to the 16th century when Angers was a Catholic stronghold and Saumur, a powerful Protestant enclave.

North of ancient Angers, the rolling countryside is veined by rivers, many dotted by *péniches* (houseboats) that drift peacefully past sleepy villages. Nearby, privately owned châteaux – such as Montgeoffroy and Serrant, le Plessis-Macé and le Plessis-Bourré – echo with long-forgotten intrigue, the moat and drawbridge now a last line of defence against tourists shooting with long lens cameras.

To the northeast of Angers, in the Loir valley (a tributary of the bigger Loire), are La Flèche, home of France's prestigious military academy, and Le Lude, which originally dates from the 15th century, and over the last 250 years has been lived in by the same family. Its beautiful, recently developed gardens host a garden festival and workshop each summer.

North of the Loire, the houses and castles are roofed in grey-blue slate, mined at Trélazé. South of the Loire, red clay roof tiles hint at the architecture of the Mediterranean. To the west, an endless sea of vines produces Muscadet, sharp as a green

The formidable façade of le Plessis-Bourré

apple. To the east, round Saumur, red and sparkling wines (*vins mousseux*) are tended in cool dark caverns that are also a temporary home to millions of mushrooms. Other caves are hidden beneath the plains round Doué-la-Fontaine, the City of Roses, to the west of which the film actor Gérard Depardieu has a vineyard. These secret attractions are matched by the little-known dessert wines of the Côteaux du Layon and the village of Clisson, an Italian style *città* deep in the French countryside, complete with its *campanile* (bell tower).

The war that raged here two centuries ago between local royalists and republicans is commemorated with monuments and the red handkerchiefs sold in souvenir shops. Living history is encapsulated at the abbeys of Solesmes and Cunault where the monks chant services in timeless plainsong. In Baugé, a small chapel is home to the famous double cross, symbol of Anjou, then of Lorraine – when the Comte d'Anjou became the Duc de Lorraine by marriage – and then of the Free France movement in World War II.

Angers

Angers straddles a river – not the Loire, the longest in France, but the Maine, the shortest. Formed by the confluence of the Loir, Mayenne and Sarthe, it flows for only 5km before emptying into the Loire, southwest of the city. Centuries ago, Angers was an important port, with ships sailing up from the Atlantic.

Today, it is also an international airport and the important link is with Paris: by TGV the French capital is only 1½ hours away from this bustling city of 260,000, with two universities and a thriving city centre.

The city dates back to a Roman settlement, founded in 14 BC as the capital of the region ruled by the Celtic Andes tribe. As the old capital of Anjou, it was the power base for leaders such as Foulques III Nerra (see p68) who, in the 11th century, built churches, a stone bridge over the river and a new settlement, La Doutre, on the western bank. The castle was built as a defence against the English, whose claim to French lands stemmed from the crowning of Henri, Comte d'Anjou, as King Henry II of England. Later wars left their mark.

The Wars of Religion saw a massacre of local Protestants in 1572. Over two centuries later, in the Revolutionary period, fighting erupted again, this time between republicans and royalists based in the nearby Vendée region to the southwest.

Not all of Angers' history is military. Its reputation for culture dates back to the 15th century and the best-loved Angevin of all: le Bon Roi René (see box). Today, the city is a centre of weaving, home to the medieval Apocalypse Tapestry and the modern *Chant du Monde*, as well as the Regional Centre for Textile Art. Although the bridges, law courts, gardens and theatre date mainly from the 19th century, the old quarter by the imposing fortress boasts photogenic medieval and Renaissance buildings, some now housing museums. On the outskirts are well-kept suburbs and modern *zones industrielles*, where computer and electronics companies are located, as well as the distillery that produces the famous orange liqueur, Cointreau, a 150-year-old local business.

LE BON ROI RENÉ (1409–80)

Good King René was never the king of France, and he was only king of Hungary, Jerusalem and Naples in name. He was, however, Comte d'Anjou.

Educated and enlightened, he loved music, literature and gardens and bequeathed The Apocalypse Tapestry to the cathedral. His huge festivals, inspired by the age of chivalry, were immensely popular. His youthful statue stands in the middle of the traffic near the château in Angers, where he was born. He died in Provence, after Anjou had been annexed by the French under King Louis XI.

Cathédrale Saint-Maurice

Standing high above the river, this compact 12th-century cathedral has no flying buttresses and no side aisles. On either side of the door are figures from the Old Testament (note the long plaits and slim waist of Esther) while higher up the façade are statues representing St Maurice and his companions.

Inside, the nave is typical of the 'Angevin Gothic' or 'Plantagenet' style. The chancel is the burial place of the Counts of Anjou, including Good King René.

The 12th- to 16th-century stained-glass windows are the glory of the cathedral. The chancel window, 15th from the left, depicts the Martyrdom of St Thomas à Becket, which took place in 1170 and so was a fairly recent event when the glass was made.
Place Freppel.

Le Château

This 13th-century fortress impresses by its sheer mass. Made of alternating bands of shale and tufa, the horizontal white and black lines emphasise the 1km-length of the perimeter wall, guarded by 17 towers. Now standing between 40 and 50m in height, they were even more dominating before the tops were dismantled during the Wars of Religion, although the original order was to demolish the entire fortress. Constructed between 1230 and 1239, the castle replaced a wooden fort built by Foulques III Nerra, who is supposed

The town of Angers was once an important port

Rose window: medieval stained glass in Angers' cathedral

to have thrown his wife from the ramparts after discovering her infidelity. Today, the peaceful ramparts support a herb garden and vines, which now grow in the former moat, and offer exceptional views of the town, the skyline and the manicured gardens within the walls.

A specially built modern gallery houses *La Tapisserie de L'Apocalypse* (The Apocalypse Tapestry), the world's largest tapestry, based on an illustrated manuscript of the Bible's *Book of Revelation*. Woven between 1373 and 1383 on the orders of Louis I of Anjou, it was 130m (426ft) long and 4.5m (15ft) high. Although the symbolism may be confusing, the overall theme is the battle between good and evil. Each of the six 'chapters' tells a story, introduced by a narrator. Gruesome scenes of death and destruction are lightened by humorous border details.

Originally, only a few panels were shown at a time, though the whole was taken to Arles and displayed for the wedding of Louis I of Anjou, father of Good King René. During the Revolution, it was cut up into more than 70 pieces and used as blankets, doormats and bed canopies; fortunately, most of the pieces were recovered and reassembled in 1848. You can appreciate the tapestries on many levels: by following the story with Bible in hand, by admiring the technical skill needed for weaving a butterfly or a horse's mane, or simply by looking at the faces whose emotions are recognisable and vivid even after 600 years. To understand the history and symbolism fully, join a tour or rent the headphones. Of the original 90 tapestries, 75 still remain, measuring 103m (338ft) in length.
Tel: 02 41 86 48 77.
www.angers.monuments-nationalix.fr.
Open: daily except public holidays.
Admission charge.

La Distillerie Cointreau (Cointreau Distillery)
Sniff the dried orange peel which flavours this famous liqueur. The one-hour guided tour shows the distilling process but the recipe remains secret.
Espace Cointreau, Carrefour Molière, St-Barthélémy. Tel: 02 41 43 25 21.
Open: mid-Jun–mid-Sept, tours daily, phone for times Sun & public holidays only. Closed: 23 Dec–2 Jan &1 May.
Admission charge.

Galerie David d'Angers

A ruined 13th-century abbey with a modern roof, hidden in the garden behind the Musée des Beaux-Arts, is the dramatic setting for plaster casts donated by the famous romantic sculptor, Pierre-Jean David (1788–1856), known as David d'Angers, after his birthplace. The casts are from statues of famous men, such as Voltaire, Gutenberg, Goethe and Balzac, many of whom are on show in the Louvre, the Panthéon and Père Lachaise Cemetery in Paris.
33–37 bis, rue Toussaint.
Tel: 02 41 05 38 90.
www.musees.angers.fr. Open: daily,
except Mon & public holidays.
Admission charge.

Maison d'Adam

Adam and Eve were removed in the French Revolution, but this half-timbered merchant's house, built around 1500, still has its carved Annunciation scene, a pelican feeding three chicks and numerous other carved figures that were there to display the owner's success. Now it is a shop selling local crafts, including tapestries.
Corner of rue Montault and place Ste-Croix. Open: Tue–Sat. Free admission.

Musée des Beaux-Arts
(Le Logis Barrault)

This atmospheric provincial art gallery has collections detailing the history of Anjou from the 12th to 14th centuries, housed in the handsome late 15th-century Logis Barrault. There is an extensive collection of 14th–16th century Renaissance 'primitive' paintings, a large number of 16th century portraits and a superb collection of 18th–19th century works of the French School.
14 rue du Musée. Tel: 02 41 05 38 00.
www.musees.angers.fr. Open: daily,
except Mon & public holidays.
Admission charge.

Musée Jean Lurçat et de la Tapisserie Contemporaine

Jean Lurçat, an Aubusson weaver, was inspired by the Apocalypse Tapestry to design the vibrant *Le Chant du Monde* (the *Song of the World*) between 1957

Gardens have replaced the water in the moat of Angers' castle

and 1966. It hangs in the 12th-century Hôpital St-Jean, in the La Doutre suburb alongside other textile works and china and porcelain pieces from the 17th–18th centuries. Nearby is the Centre Regional d'Art Textile where visitors can watch weavers at work. The city centre contains many workshops.
Museum: 4 boulevard Arago. Tel: 02 41 24 18 45. Open: daily, except Mon & public holidays. Admission charge.

Ancenis

Ancenis was once an important port for shipping wine. Today, the town is dominated by the 500m- (1,640ft) long suspension bridge over the Loire. The arms of Brittany and Anjou displayed at opposite ends recall the ancient boundary. Little more than the twin turrets and the Renaissance Grand Logis (hall) remain of the castle.

Liré

Two kilometres south of Ancenis, the Musée Joachim-Du-Bellay honours the 16th-century poet who was born here in 1522. In the cellar there is also a small museum of wine.
*Tel: 02 40 09 04 13. www.musee-du-bellay.fr.st. Open: Mar–Jun & Sept–Oct Tue–Fri, Jul–Aug Tue–Sun.
Admission charge.
Ancenis is 45km (28 miles) west of Angers on the north bank of the Loire.*

Baugé

The treasure here is not the 15th-century château but a medieval crucifix

---

THE VENDÉE WARS (1793–1796)

Not everyone saw the French Revolution as a liberating force. South-west of Angers, the people of the Vendée region took up arms in support of the king. Blood-red handkerchiefs were worn as a badge of courage by les Blancs (the Whites, or royalists) and windmill sails were used to send messages

This bloody war produced its heroes. Napoleon Bonaparte, a general of the republican army, called the Vendée the 'land of the giants' after 3,000 peasants held off his army of 25,000. Though defeated at Cholet, the royalist General Bonchamps begged his men not to massacre 5,000 captured republicans, held at St-Florent-le-Vieil, in revenge.

Two centuries on, reminders of the wars remain. The symbol of the Vendée – two hearts under a cross and crown – stands for loyalty to God and king. Some villages still resolutely ignore the Bastille Day celebrations of 14 July.

---

studded with gold and gems, housed in a former chapel that was part of an 18th-century hospice. *La Vraie Croix* (The True Cross) is made from a piece of the cross of Christ, which was brought back from the Holy Land in 1241. Hidden in Angers during the Hundred Years War (1337–1453) and moved to Baugé during the Revolution (1789), it became the emblem of the Dukes of Anjou, who became Dukes of Lorraine after King René married Isabelle of Lorraine. In 1940, General de Gaulle made it the symbol of Free France.
Chapelle des Filles du Coeur de Marie, 8 rue de la Girouardière. Tel: 02 41 89 12 20. Open: Wed–Mon afternoons. Donation requested.

Château de Baugé

Baugé is a Renaissance château that was much favoured by the Duc d'Anjou. It also houses the Musée d'Art et Histoire. *Tel: 02 41 84 00 74. www.chateaubauge.com. Open: Apr–Sept daily, Feb–Apr & Sept–Oct Wed–Sun, visit by guided tour only. Admission charge. Baugé is 40km (25 miles) east of Angers on the D766.*

Château de Boumois

This lovely 16th-century château was the birthplace of Captain Aristide Dupetit-Thouars (1760–98). Horribly mutilated at the Battle of the Nile in 1798, he ordered his sailors to put his bleeding torso into a barrel of bran on the quarterdeck of his ship, the *Tonnant*, so that he could carry on with the battle, with no thought of surrender. The château contains mementoes of the Dupetit-Thouars family, and a fine full-length portrait of Queen Elizabeth I of England. *45km (28 miles) southeast of Angers on the north bank of the Loire, near Saint-Martin-de-la-Place. Tel: 02 41 38 43 16. Open: Jul–mid-Aug Wed–Mon. Admission charge.*

Château de Brissac

'*Si je n'étais dauphin, je voudrais être Brissac,*' sighed the future King Henri II in 1542 ('If I weren't heir to the throne, I'd like to be a Brissac.'). The Dukes of Brissac still call this home – all 204 rooms of it. Set on the Aubance River, two chunks of the original 15th-century castle guard the densely decorated *pavillon* (central façade). The interior is fascinating and features a red and gold theatre built for an ancestor with a fine voice, a portrait of

Rich mixture: Boumois architecture is part-Gothic, part-Renaissance

Tall story: the Château de Brissac towers a full seven storeys high

the famous Veuve (Widow) Clicquot, who gave her name to a brand of Champagne, and a number of original ceiling paintings and 17th-century tapestries. The Dukes of Brissac gained their title as a reward for surrendering Paris to King Henri IV in 1594, thus helping to bring an end to the Wars of Religion. The estate vineyards produce good quality Anjou-village wine.
20km (12 miles) southeast of Angers off the D748. Tel: 02 41 91 22 21. www.chateau-brissac.fr. Open: Jul & Aug daily 9am–7pm; Apr–Jun & Sept–Oct Tue–Sun; Nov–Mar school holidays only. Admission charge.

Cholet

Cholet today is a centre for the manufacture of high-quality clothes. The town was razed to the ground in 1794 during the brief and bloody Vendée Wars (*see p28*) but the 'double red heart' badge of the region is still worn with pride and symbolic red handkerchiefs are sold in souvenir shops. Learn about the royalist cause in the **Art and History Museum**.
58km (36 miles) southwest of Angers on the N160. Musée d'Art et d'Histoire: 27 Ave de l'Abreuvoir. Tel: 02 41 49 29 00. www.ville-cholet.fr. Open: Wed–Sun & public holidays. Admission charge.

Clisson

'A little bit of Italy on the Sèvre River' is one reaction to the town's square bell towers, its loggias and its Roman-tile roofs. After fire destroyed the town during the Vendée Wars of 1794, two locals engaged the sculptor-architect Frédéric Lemot to rebuild their town. Survivors of the fire include the handsome 15th-century covered market, a couple of bridges and the castle ruins. The summer music festival is first class.
90km (55 miles) southwest of Angers on the D763.

Cunault

Listen to Gregorian chant at Sunday Mass to appreciate the atmosphere of this Romanesque priory church, built by 12th- and 13th-century Benedictine monks on the bank of the Loire. Pilgrims can surely not have been able to decipher the carvings high up on the 223 pillars – bring binoculars if you want to do so. The usually quiet hamlet bustles with a craft market on Sunday mornings in summer.
40km (25 miles) southeast of Angers on the south bank of the Loire.

Doué-la-Fontaine

Doué is nicknamed La Cité des Roses (the City of Roses) because over eight million stems are grown here annually and shipped all over Europe. Some 500 varieties are found in the Parc Foulon and the air is scented by 100,000 blooms during the Journées de la Rose, the annual rose festival, in mid-July. The rose show takes place in a disused limestone quarry, now an amphitheatre; another series of old quarries has an unusually fine zoo (*see p153*). In the former stables of a long-gone château is the **Musée des Commerces Anciens**, a museum of village shops. Much more interesting than it sounds, you can see how chemists once made pills by hand and find out why *tabacs* (tobacconists' shops) have a *carotte* (carrot-shaped sign) outside.

40km (25 miles) southeast of Angers on the D761. Musée des Commerces Anciens: Ecuries Foulon-Soulanger. Tel: 02 41 59 28 23. Open: May–Sept daily; Mar, Apr & Oct Tue–Sun. Admission charge.

La Flèche

'*J'étais fléchois avant d'avoir été béarnais*' ('I was from La Flèche before I was from Béarn'), insisted King Henri IV, who was conceived here in 1553 but born in Pau, in the south of France. In 1604, he founded the town's Jesuit college where his heart, along with that of his wife, Marie de'Medici, were interred in the chapel. Although their remains were exhumed and burnt during the French

Clisson's Italianate viaduct

Revolution, the ashes were later found and are now set in a heart-shaped urn in the north transept. One of the college's first pupils was the philosopher René Descartes (1596–1650). When the Jesuits were expelled from France, the building became a military academy, gaining its present reputation after Napoleon moved the Prytanée de St-Cyr military institution here in 1808. Many of the pupils go on to pursue a military career, and the graduates include over 800 generals.

52km (32 miles) northeast of Angers on the N23. Entrance on rue du Collège. Tel: 02 43 48 59 06. Open: Jul & Aug daily. Admission charge. Proof of identity required for admission.

Château de Goulaine

The Marquis de Goulaine's family have lived here for 1,000 years; the current château, however, dates back merely to the 15th century. Rooms such as the Salon Bleu are richly decorated and gleam with gilt. Stroll through the conservatory among hundreds of live tropical butterflies.

90km (56 miles) southwest of Angers off the N249, 11km (7 miles) east of Nantes.

The Château de Montreuil-Bellay dominates the River Thouët

Tel: 02 40 54 91 42. www.chateau.goulaine.online.fr. Open: Easter–Oct weekends & public holidays; mid-Jun–mid-Sept daily. Admission charge.

Louresse-Rochemenier

Signposted as the Village Troglodytique de Rochemenier, this settlement consisted almost entirely of underground dwellings (*see pp72–3*), carved out of the chalky limestone, until the 1930s, when the villagers built the present above-ground houses. The sunken farmsteads, houses and chapel have now been restored and a small museum shows the unromantic reality of underground life a century ago. An underground restaurant serves traditional *fouaces* (hot bread) straight from the oven.

40km (25 miles) southeast of Angers. Tel: 02 41 59 18 13. www.troglodyte.com. Open: Apr–Oct daily. Admission charge.

Malicorne-sur-Sarthe

Pottery has been made here since Roman times, and the yellow or blue-patterned Malicorne pots, often depicting birds, are famous throughout France. This former pottery workshop has recently been converted and now houses the 'Espace Faience'. The collection includes local pottery dating from the 18th century. A short film explains the potters' art, from the choice of the raw material, and the tools used, through to the final decoration.

53km (33 miles) northeast of Angers on the D23. Tel: 02 43 48 07 17. Open: Easter–Oct daily; winter Wed–Mon.

Château de Montgeoffroy

The wrought-iron gates fronting this charming château are crowned by the entwined initials of the de Contades family, owners of the Montgeoffroy estate since 1616. The 16th-century castle was remodelled by the Marshal de Contades in 1775 and scarcely anything has changed inside since – the fine furnishings, carpets and paintings remain in their original positions, giving an excellent idea of aristocratic life in the 18th century.

20km (12 miles) east of Angers off the N147 near Mazé. Tel: 02 41 80 60 02. Open: mid-Mar–mid-Nov daily. Admission charge.

Château de Montreuil-Bellay

This town on the Thouët River is dwarfed by its massive 17-towered château with a reputation for impregnability. Like many other Loire Valley châteaux, it was revamped in the 15th century (originally built in 1025).

The Harcourt family put in Turkish baths, better kitchens, 18 spiral staircases and a new chapel where frescoed angels, playing lutes and trumpets, flutter across the ceiling. On the front of the altar, a carving depicts a pregnant Virgin Mary meeting her cousin. Unlike some castles, the rooms are elegant and liveable. One of the most magnificent rooms in the château is the huge medieval kitchen with its central chimney and 18th-century cooking equipment. Equally impressive are the vaulted wine cellars, where the Confrérie de Sacavins (Brotherhood of Wine Growers) used to meet.

50km (31 miles) southeast of Angers on the N147. Tel: 02 41 52 33 06. Open: Apr–Jun & Sept–Oct Wed–Mon; Jul–Aug daily. Admission charge.

Nantes and nearby

The city that dominates the mouth of the Loire was traditionally the capital of Brittany. After the Revolution, it became the capital of the Loire-Atlantique region, and now it is the capital of the five disparate *départements* that make up the Pays de la Loire. After stagnating for most of this century, France's seventh largest city has been revived, thanks to a bold programme of expansion and modernisation, carried out over the last 20 years.

Historically, Nantes was fought over by the French and the Breton dukes until Anne of Brittany, who was born here, married King Charles VIII, bringing Brittany under French rule in

the 15th century. Nantes went on to become the country's largest port, made wealthy by the trade in slaves, sugar, rum and cotton. Decline followed the building of better facilities at nearby Saint-Nazaire, though not before a young Jules Verne was inspired by the early 19th-century dockside to begin writing his adventure stories (he once ran away to sea, but only sailed downriver as far as Paimboeuf, now a pleasant little fishing harbour 40km (25 miles) to the west).

Around the river's mouth, the countryside is open and flat. The Lac de Grand-Lieu (to the north of the city) and the marshy Grande Brière

(*Cont. on p38*)

Nantes' stunning cathedral

Walk: old Angers

Much of old Angers has been pedestrianised, so a stroll through the heart of this 'city of art and history' is particularly enjoyable.

Allow one hour.

Start at the tourist office in front of the castle (place du Président Kennedy). Turn right on rue Toussaint, known for its antique shops. The brick and stone wall on the left was built by the Romans some 1,800 years ago.

1 Abbaye de Toussaint

On the right-hand side (no 37) is an entrance to a former monastic courtyard. Turn left and walk to what remains of the 13th-century abbey church. Its dramatic modern glass roof soars above sculptures in the

Galerie David d'Angers (*see p27*).
Climb the steps and turn right, continuing along rue Toussaint. Number 25, 'built by knowledge and fortified by wisdom', was restored in 1588. Turn right on the cobbled rue du Musée.

2 Musée des Beaux-Arts

Step into the courtyard on the right and look up to see late 15th-century gargoyles. Built as a private mansion, it was once Le Logis Barrault (*see p27*). *Continue along rue du Musée, noting the mix of black slate and white limestone in*

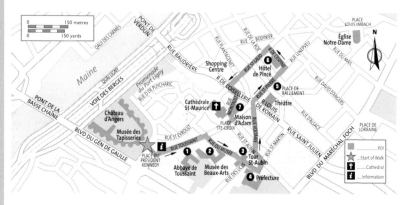

the wall. The bridge overhead linked two seminaries, one in the mansion, the other in the church of St Eloi.

3 Tour Saint-Aubin

The 55m- (180ft) high 12th-century belfry (and the cloister in the Préfecture) are all that remain of the powerful Benedictine Abbey of St Aubin founded in the 6th century. The tower originally stood outside the city walls; the opening, 4m (13ft) up, was reached by a ladder, which was then drawn up for safety.

Cross rue des Lices, where knights once held tournaments, and enter the Mail de la Préfecture.

4 Préfecture

This is the headquarters of the *département* of Maine-et-Loire. Members of the public may go in to see the remarkable Romanesque cloister with its sculptures and its frescoes of *David and Goliath*, and *Herod and the Three Kings*.

Exit on rue St-Martin and turn left on rue St-Aubin, looking up to see the cathedral's towers. Turn right at the red British telephone box on rue Voltaire. Turn right on rue St-Pierre.

5 Place de Ralliement

Some say this was the site of patriotic rallies during the French Revolution, others that the crowds met to watch executions at the guillotine. Entertainment is now provided in the theatre, built in 1871 and recently restored. The façade is decorated with busts of France's famous French

playwrights, such as Molière, Racine and Corneille.

Continue along rue Lenepveu. Turn left on rue de l'Espine, named after the architect of the Hôtel de Pincé

6 Hôtel de Pincé

Gargoyles and foliage carvings decorate this 16th-century mansion, now the Turpin de Crissé Museum of Greek, Etruscan and Egyptian antiquities, and Japanese and Chinese art.

Turn left again on rue St-Laud. Stop at no 21 to see the 15th-century carvings of Adam and Eve, plus a beast swallowing a bear. Number 38, in delightful Art Nouveau style, was once a brothel. Pass the modern shopping centre and turn left on rue de l'Oisellerie, pausing to admire the three old houses. On the right is the former bishop's palace. Turn right on rue Montault.

7 Maison d'Adam

Heavily timbered gables were a sign of wealth; the decoration is in the flamboyant Gothic style. Spot the pelican feeding its chicks, Samson fighting the lion and the man with three testicles (*see p27*).

The walk ends in the place Ste-Croix where you can visit the cathedral (see p25).

The Musée des Beaux-Arts, Angers

By boat: the Mayenne River

Although boating on the Mayenne is popular, this particular stretch of the river is remarkably unspoilt.

Allow 2 days for the return journey, and 1 day if you arrange for your boat to be collected at the end of the one-way journey.

1 Grez-Neuville

As well as a small island, old mill and a weir, this pretty village has a marina full of *pénichettes* – cruising boats with wide decks, guard rails and a practical wheel house, set well back. Rent them from L'Anjou Plaisance; bicycles are usually supplied with the boats (*tel: 02 43 95 14 42; www.anjou-navigation.com*). No permit is required. *Head upstream (north), passing the first lock (no 42) on the left. After a few minutes, the Oudon River also flows in from the left. Head beneath the bridge at the river junction, and up the Oudon for 1.5km (1 mile).*

Grez-Neuville is a good starting point for exploring the Mayenne River

2 Le Lion d'Angers

On the right, the Isle-Briand is one of France's best-known national studs with 75 thoroughbred stallions, plus a fine race course. Watch for horses in training. (*Guided visits in the afternoon, tel: 02 41 18 05 00.*)
Return to the Mayenne, continue upstream.

3 Montreuil-sur-Maine

Thick trees line both banks, but at Montreuil, the church spire pokes out above the greenery.
The second lock (no 41) is at Montreuil, and a small, elegant country house peeks through the trees on the left. The third lock (no 40), at La Roche Chambellay, takes boats to the left, between the bank and a small island. Look across the fields to the church spire in Chambellay.

4 Chambellay

A distinctive five-arched bridge carries the D290 across the river. Some enthusiasts moor here and pedal 2km (1 mile) to look at the 15th-century

Château de Bois-Montbourcher (not open to the public). Others pop into the church to see the frescoes.
Continue upstream.

5 Chenillé-Changé

This base for cruising boats is lit up at night and boasts of being voted France's prettiest 'flowery' village in 1999 and the region's most charming village in 2001. Even the pink lock-keeper's cottage has a manicured garden. The old watermill still functions, although it is now a restaurant, La Table du Meunier.
Continue upstream for about 3km (2 miles) to La Jaille-Yvon.

6 La Jaille-Yvon

This village is hidden from view on a bluff, 50m above the water. From the campsite at the foot of the cliff, climb up to the 11th-century church for a sweeping view over the countryside.
Continue upstream via lock no 38, past the château at Le Port-Joulain, a popular stretch for water-skiers.

7 Daon

Everyone seems to be having fun in this little resort where the flags of eight nations flap on the modern bridge. L'Embarcadère restaurant, on the water, specialises in grilled meat and fish.
Beyond Daon, the lock at Formusson (no 37) has charts showing local bird life. Now the Mayenne narrows to form an oxbow bend, with chestnuts and hazels hiding the Château de Magnanne on the left bank.

8 Ménil

In this charming hamlet, an old-fashioned, hand-powered *bac* (ferry) takes pedestrians and bicycles to and fro.
Three more locks (nos 36, 35 & 34) lead into the affluent town of Château-Gontier.

9 Château-Gontier

Handsome quayside gardens greet boaters; even the tourist office is housed in a converted boat. The 11th-century church of St-Jean-Baptiste is a treasure and the old town has many half-timbered houses.
Continue upstream to the rural peace of Mirwault, where the Hostellerie de Mirwault is a fine place to celebrate the halfway point, or the end, of the journey.

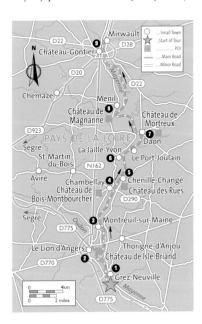

nature park (to the west), are a paradise for birdwatchers. Few people live here now: traditional peat-cutting is restricted to a few days every August and the once-profitable salt-pans have been converted to fish and oyster farms.

For many visitors the most memorable sight within the Nantes area is the 3.5km- (2-mile) long Saint-Nazaire bridge, which soars 60m above the Loire and links Saint-Nazaire to Saint-Brévin across the mouth of the river. Even Jules Verne did not anticipate this exhilarating experience.

Cathédrale Saint-Pierre-et-Saint-Paul

This flamboyant Gothic cathedral took more than four centuries to complete. Buried in the right-hand transept is François III, father of Anne of Brittany, who lies in a masterfully sculpted white marble tomb.
Place St Pierre. Open daily.

Cité des Métiers de Tradition

When villagers stop weaving or making clogs and wine the old-fashioned way, their tools are usually thrown out. Luckily, the locals here kept their tools and opened an imaginative crafts museum representing some 50 trades. A 'village street' shows the younger generation how the blacksmith and candle-maker worked. Everything comes to life in July and August when live crafts demonstrations are given. Entertaining as well as educational for youngsters.

26km (16 miles) southwest of Angers off the N160 and D170. Tel: 02 41 78 24 08. Open: Apr & Sept Tue–Sun afternoons only; May–Aug daily except Sat & Sun mornings. Admission charge.

Château des Ducs de Bretagne

This majestic château, built in the style of the Château of Angers, with curtain walls and round bastions, is the birthplace of Anne of Brittany. Anne married her second husband, Louis XII, in 1499 in the château chapel, and the Edict of Nantes was signed here in 1598 by Henri IV. François II, Anne's father built most of this château but the architecture of the Grand Logis has clearly been influenced by Anne, with its Flamboyant and Renaissance styles. Beautifully restored, the château now houses a revolutionary museum revealing the history of the château, the city and the region. Historical exhibits and multimedia presentations bring the whole lot to life.
Place Marc Elder. Tel: 02 40 41 56 56. www.chateau-nantes.fr. Open: daily, low season Wed–Sun. Admission charge.

Château du Plessis-Macé

Plessis is a local term meaning 'palisade'. Unlike le Plessis-Bourré, built in just one architectural style, Macé is a mixture, accentuated by dark and light stone. The original 11th-century fortress was partially destroyed during the Hundred Years War; the keep and oak-panelled chapel are 15th- and 16th-century additions. Kings Louis XI,

THE ENGLISH CONNECTION

Like Normandy, the Loire's historical links with England date from the time of William the Conqueror, crowned King of England in 1066. His great-grandson, Henri Plantagenet, ruled Normandy, Anjou, Touraine and Maine. After marrying Eleanor of Aquitaine (*see p64*), he controlled over half of France. In 1154, he became King Henry II of England. His death gave impetus to the rivalry between the monarchs of France and England that culminated in the Hundred Years War, much of it fought in the Loire Valley. A turning point came when Jeanne d'Arc led the French to victory at Orléans in 1429. Even so, the English continued to rule parts of France until the loss of Calais in 1558, and did not finally cede their claims to French territory until 1801.

Charles VII, François I and Henri IV all stayed here, but the buildings were subsequently used as a farm for 200 years, and they fell into a state of near ruin until rescued and restored by the Countess Theobold Walsh in the 1870s (*see* Château de Serrant, *p42*).
14km (8 miles) northwest of Angers off the N162. Tel: 02 41 32 67 93. Open: Jul & Aug all day; Mar–Jun & Sept–Nov Wed–Sun afternoons. Admission charge.

Île de Nantes

The 5km- (3-mile) long Île de Nantes, south of the centre, used to be home to the city docks and shipbuilding industry. Although two huge cranes, some storehouses and dockyard offices have been preserved, the area is now home to a creative group, inspired by Jules Verne, who are bringing giant sea creatures to life on the Mondes Marin Carousel, creating a huge steel tree, the *arbre aux herons*, complete with mechanical herons; and offering rides on the 12m- (39ft) high grand elephant – a mechanical marvel that patrols the area, trumpeting and spraying passers-by.
*Galerie des Machines de l'Île.
Tel: 08 10 12 12 25. www.lesmachines-nantes.fr. Open: Feb–Dec.*

Musée des Beaux Arts

The fine 19th-century, neoclassical museum is indicative of Nantes' wealth and status. Inside is a collection of sculptures and thousands of paintings from the 13th to 19th centuries, acquired by diplomat and art collector François Cacault. The collection continues to swell with more modern additions.
*10 rue Georges Clémenceau.
Tel: 02 51 17 45 00. Open: Wed–Mon. Admission charge.*

Fishing boats in front of the Pont de St-Nazaire

Château life

The Château du Plessis-Bourré, north of Angers was built in just seven years, so it is easy to follow the plan of the building and understand how the rooms were actually used. The 2m- (6ft) thick walls and 44m- (144ft) high *donjon* (keep) show that this was still, in part, a fortress complete with a gatehouse and four flanking towers, despite its early-Renaissance comforts.

Moats and bridges

The château was built on a terrace, and was originally protected by three moats. At the end of the 43m- (141ft) long arched bridge, the restored drawbridge can be raised or lowered by one person in seconds, thanks to the 900kg (2,000lbs) counterbalance.

The courtyard

Less austere than the exterior, the courtyard shows the influence of Renaissance ideas. On the west side, a covered walkway connects the main lodgings and the chapel; opposite are the servants' quarters and kitchens. The courtyard was large enough to host outdoor feasts, with musicians and jesters to entertain the guests.

Living quarters

The height of the Logis Seigneurial (master's lodging) was designed to impress. On the ground floor, the Vestibule d'Honneur (entrance hall) has a massive fireplace, and the walls would have been hung with tapestries for additional insulation. In the

Despite its history and antiques, Château du Plessis-Bourré is still a family home

One of the many sumptuous castle bedchambers

Louis XVI room, 18th-century wood-panelling, painted the fashionable grey of the period, has replaced tapestry. The Grand Salon has fine 18th-century carvings on the walls but the Salle de Parlement (the vaulted ceremonial room) dates from an earlier period, when King Charles VIII and his sister, the regent Anne de Beaujeu, met ambassadors from Hungary here in 1487. The arms of the various monarchs who visited Plessis-Bourré, carved on the back of the door, show the owners' loyalty to the crown.

Upstairs, the Salle des Gardes was not actually the guard room. Instead, this heavily decorated room was the library of the owner Jean Bourré, whose fascination with alchemy prompted the allegorical figures painted on the 24 ceiling panels. Next door, the 19th-century Empire Room claims to have the only bed that Napoleon never slept in. The 35m-(100ft) long Gallery was used for meeting, talking and doing business. At one end, the tiny loggia allowed the owner to attend Mass without mixing with the servants in the chapel below.

Chapel of St Anne

All châteaux had their own chapel, with their own priests, and the encircled red crosses here indicate that this one is still consecrated. The obligatory statue of the local hero, St Martin, is in one corner.

Le Passage Pommeraye

Built in 1843 this is the only passage classed as a historic monument. This glass-covered neoclassical passage combining columns, statues, a canopy of glass and wrought iron and oak steps, has elegant shops on three floors. *Located between rue Grébillon and the rue de la Fosse.*

Sablé-sur-Sarthe

The Erve River joins the Sarthe here, and a stretch of canalised river has been turned into a marina where holiday craft can be hired. There is also a river boat for short cruises along the Sarthe. Above stands the proud château where 19th-century inventor Charles Cros conducted his experiments. It now houses an annexe of the National Library of France. The attractive town is known for its shortbread-like biscuits. *64km (40 miles) northeast of Angers off the A11 and D306.*

One of the sluices on the Sarthe

Saint-Florent-le-Vieil

The small town perched above the Loire has two claims to fame: it is the place where the Vendée Wars began in 1793 and it is the resting place of the royalist leader, General Bonchamps (*see p28*). His romantic white marble effigy in the 18th-century church standing on a hill above the old town was a moving 'thank you' from the sculptor, David d'Angers, whose father was one of 5,000 prisoners saved from slaughter by Bonchamps. Each year the town hosts a music festival at the end of June and July.
42km (26 miles) west of Angers off the N23 and D752. Tel: 02 41 72 62 32. For festival details. www.ville-saintflorentlevieil.fr

Saint-Georges-sur-Loire
Château de Serrant

This château is one of two in the region (*see* Château du Plessis-Macé, *pp39–40*) associated with the Walsh family (Irish Jacobites descended from Captain Francis Walsh) who helped King James II escape to France when he was deposed from the English throne by William III of Orange in 1688. Walsh settled in Nantes and grew rich as a merchant and shipowner. His son, Antoine, subsequently provided the frigate, *La Doutelle*, used by Bonnie Prince Charlie in 1745 for his disastrous attempt to retake the Scottish and English thrones. In 1749, the Walsh family bought this château, and though it passed to the family of

Messing about on the river: the marina at Sablé-sur-Sarthe

the present owner, Prince Jean-Charles de Ligne, in 1830, there are reminders of the Walsh connection in the magnificent library, with its 12,000 volumes. Begun in 1546, it took another 200 years to complete the château, but the builders remained faithful to the original plan. The result is a gem of geometry – balanced and photogenic – with gravelled paths, a moat and domed turrets. The furnishings are exceptional, so this château is well worth seeing inside, especially the restored kitchen.

1km (¹/₂ mile) northeast of St-Georges-sur-Loire. Tel: 02 41 39 13 01. www.chateau-serrant.net. Open: Mar–Nov Wed–Mon; Jul & Aug daily. Admission charge.

St-Georges-sur-Loire is 18km (11 miles) west of Angers on the N23.

Saint-Hilaire-St-Florent

Wedged between tufa cliffs and the Thouët River, this is the main production centre for sparkling Saumur wine. Many of the labyrinthine rock galleries where the wine is stored can be visited (*see pp144–5*). Underground there is both a **museum of mushrooms** (*see p151*) and a 'parc miniature' where scaled-down copies of churches, villages and châteaux found in the Loire Valley have been sculpted into the limestone. On the plateau above the town is the famous national riding school, L'École Nationale d'Equitation (*see pp154–5*). *48km (30 miles) southeast of Angers on the D751. Musée du Champignon, La Houssaye. Tel: 02 41 50 31 55. www.musee-du-champignon.com*

Saint-Lambert-du-Lattay

This unremarkable village is the production centre for the Côteaux du Layon dessert wine. All is explained in the small **museum**.
15km (9 miles) southwest of Angers on the N160. Musée de la Vigne et du Vin d'Anjou. Tel: 02 41 78 42 75.
(*Cont. on p46*)

By bike: the Layon Valley

The Layon is a relatively unknown tributary of the Loire; local vineyards produce Côteaux du Layon, sweet white wines drunk by the locals as an aperitif, with dessert or even right through a meal. Although not long, this is a testing route, best done by mountain bike.

Allow half a day, longer if you take the optional canoe trip on the Layon River.

Start from St-Lambert-du-Lattay, where the tourist office (tel: 02 41 78 44 26) not only rents out bicycles but has also mapped out several trails, which are marked with red, green or blue arrows.

1 Saint-Lambert-du-Lattay

Straddling the busy N160, this village boasts 50 winegrowers whose skills are explained in the Musée de la Vigne et du Vin d'Anjou (*see p43*). Nearby, the Maison du Vin sells the local red, white

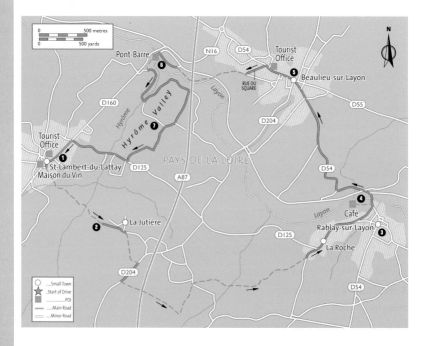

and rosé wines, and the sweet Côteaux du Layon (*open: Apr–Oct*).

Start in the main square by the Maison du Vin. Follow markers for the tourist office's 'red route' to La Roche.

2 The vineyards

The trail descends steeply past a pond and campsite; follow the arrows pointing to a rough path through the vines. Note the information board explaining the varieties of grapes grown here, including *groslot* for making Rosé d'Anjou.

Cross the bridge. Except for birdsong and the distant church clock, silence reigns. The path passes oak trees and nettles, blackthorn and thistle; continue through vineyards and maize fields. Beyond the hamlet of La Roche, leave the tourist board's route and follow signs to Rablay-sur-Layon.

3 Rablay-sur-Layon

This 'artists' community', home to various painters, sculptors and artisans, remains pleasantly uncommercial, with Le Mail, an atmospheric small square, and an ancient Maison de la Dîme (tithe house).

Return to the tourist board route at the edge of La Roche. At the side of the building on the right, signposted, 'Domaine des Quarres, Vignoble Bidet', take the rough trail down to the valley floor.

4 From Pedal to Paddle

Follow the Layon River; stop and rest on the bank and watch the boats glide upstream. (For boat trips, *tel: 02 41 78 52 98* at St-Aubin de Luigné.)

Resume the cycle ride, crossing the bridge. Do not turn off on to the 'red route'. Follow the D54 up the steep hill to Beaulieu-sur-Layon.

5 Beaulieu-sur-Layon

This ancient village thrived in the 19th century, thanks to nearby coal mines and limeworks; now it is known for its wines and flowers.

Just beyond the tourist office, turn sharp left on the rue du Square. Pick up the 'red route' again, heading back down to the river. Turn right and follow the bankside path to the old bridge.

6 Pont-Barre

'*Ici commence le pays de la Guerre des Géants*' (The land of the Giants' War starts here) – so says the plaque commemorating the 2,000 soldiers who died here on 19 September 1793, in the Vendée Wars (*see p28*). The peasant-soldiers were dubbed 'the Giants' by Napoleon Bonaparte when 3,000 of them defeated his 25,000-strong army.

Cross the bridge and join the 'green route' into the Hyrôme valley.

7 Hyrôme Valley

After about 1km ($\frac{1}{2}$ mile), on the left, there is a carved stone tablet under a chestnut tree recalling the days when eight watermills dotted the banks of the river. Now the valley is enjoyed by nature lovers, ramblers and cyclists.

Return to St-Lambert via the D125.

By bike: the Layon Valley

*www.mvvanjou.com Open: Apr–Jun,
Sept–Oct weekends & public holidays
2.30–6.30pm; Jul & Aug daily
11am–1pm, 3–7pm. Admission charge.*

Saumur

Saumur became an important
Protestant enclave after the ambitious
16th-century governor Duplessis-
Mornay (nicknamed 'the Huguenot
pope') founded a college that attracted
Protestants from all over Europe.
Industrious Huguenot businessmen
soon followed and the city prospered
until the revocation of the Edict of
Nantes (*see p57*), when much of the
population fled. The arrival of the
cavalry (*see p48*) brought a revival.
Since then wine, mushrooms and the
army have underpinned the economy.
With its old quarter, its grandiose and
newly renovated town hall, its small
shops and its château, Saumur is
one of the most attractive towns in
the region.

Le Château

Perched on a limestone plinth, Saumur's
fairy-tale style medieval fortress enjoys
views that stretch for 20km (12 miles)
up, down and across the Loire Valley.
Horses once clattered up the steep
drawbridge; the smooth side ramp was
for barrels. Inside are small museums of
ceramics, furniture and religious art.
Twenty-four spiral steps down in the
gloom is a real dungeon, while up under
the eaves is an equestrian museum, with
saddles from Iran to Mexico, plus

Slate mining: the Trélazé coat of arms

uniforms, boots weighing 2kg each and
even an equine skeleton.
*Tel: 02 41 40 24 40. www.ville-saumur.fr.
Open: daily. Closed: Nov–Mar on Tue.
Admission charge.*

Le Dolmen de Bagneux

The Dolmen of Bagneux is one of
Europe's largest prehistoric chamber
tombs, but the setting, in a garden with
entry via a café, is less than impressive.
*56 rue de Dolmen, Bagneux. Tel: 02 41
50 23 02. www.saumur-dolmen.com.
Open: daily. Closed: Sept–Jun on Wed.
Admission charge.*

Notre-Dame de Nantilly

This fine 12th-century Romanesque
church is hung with 15th- to 17th-
century tapestries depicting scenes
from the lives of Christ and the Virgin.
Also notable is the epitaph to Lady
Thyphaine, supposedly composed by
Good King Réné (*see p24*) as a tribute
to his wet-nurse.
rue de Nantilly.

Musée des Blindés (Tank Museum) and Musée de la Cavalerie (Cavalry Museum)

See p155.

Solesmes Abbey

This Benedictine abbey, founded in 1010, was closed during the Revolution but reoccupied by a new community of monks in 1833, to become the headquarters of the French Benedictines in 1837 and a major force in the revival of the Gregorian chant. With its 50m-(164ft) high walls, it looks more like a fortress than a retreat but the medieval style is largely a 19th-century creation. Only the abbey church of St-Pierre is open to the public. In the transept are the very fine 16th-century sculptural groups known as the 'Solesmes Saints'. These depict scenes from the life of the Virgin. Jean Bougler, the 16th-century prior who commissioned the work, is depicted in the crowded Entombment scene, holding the Virgin's shroud.

65km (40 miles) northeast of Angers off the A11 and D306, not far from Sablé. Tel: 02 43 95 03 08. www.solesmes.com. Open: daily, with services at 10am & Vespers between 4 & 5.30pm depending on season. Donation appreciated.

Trélazé

For centuries, the slate centre of France provided roofing for cathedrals and châteaux. Undercut by cheaper competition, slate is quarried nowadays only for renovating historic buildings. At the Slate Museum, retired *ardoisiers* (slate workers), wearing clogs on their feet and cloths round their legs, demonstrate how to convert a ton of rock into grey-blue wafers.

5km (3 miles) southeast of Angers off the D952. Musée de l'Ardoise. Tel: 02 41 69 04 71. Open: Jul–mid-Sept Tue–Sun 2pm; mid-Sept–Jun Sun & public holidays only 2pm. Admission charge.

Bird's-eye view: the town of Saumur from the château ramparts

Saumur's horses

The partnership of Saumur and horses dates back to the 16th century when the Protestant university opened and a Monsieur de St-Vual set up a riding academy alongside. Then, when the French cavalry was reorganised by the Duke de Choiseul, in 1763, he chose Saumur as the site of the new training school for officers.

The French Revolution put a temporary stop to this elitism, but the Royal School of Cavalry reopened early in the 19th century, with the Cadre Noir squad of officers formed in 1814. An early riding master designed the handsome all-black uniform that is still worn today, trimmed with gold braid and topped

Saumur has strong claims to be the equestrian capital of France

April and September, thousands also watch the Reprise du Manège, a balletic dressage, and the Reprise des Sauteurs, when the horses and riders perform a series of gravity-defying jumps, similar to a gymnast's floor exercises. You don't have to be an equine enthusiast to admire the skills of the horses, or of the men and women, who ride without the benefit of stirrups.

Since 1972, the school (now the École Nationale d'Equitation) has come under the government's Sports' Ministry, and among the 450 horses and 200 pupils are Olympic show-jumpers and three-day event horses, carriage drivers and dressage riders, all being trained under the watchful eye of 45 staff, 20 of whom are members of the illustrious Cadre Noir.

Even if you can't see horses in action, you can always visit the Musée de la Cavalerie, tracing the history of the French cavalry from 1445 to the present day through period illustrations, paintings, well-preserved uniforms and full-size equine models.

A rider showing off her skills

by a *lampion* (cocked hat). In 1828, the young officers celebrated their graduation for the first time with a public exhibition of equestrian skill, known as the carrousel.

The carrousel is still the most famous of the displays but, between

ÉCOLE NATIONALE D'EQUITATION

Tel: 02 41 53 50 60. www.cadrenoir.fr
Open: mid Feb–Nov daily except Sat pm, Sun & Mon am & public holidays.
Telephone for tours and performance times.
Admission charge.

West Central Loire

Most of the Loire Valley's famous châteaux are located in this region, even if they are on other rivers, such as the Cher, the Indre and the Vienne. Some date back 900 years to the era of Foulques III Nerra, Comte d'Anjou, who was a prolific builder of fortresses (see p68). In later centuries, these châteaux were strengthened as protection against the English, particularly during the Hundred Years War.

The end of the war, in 1453, marked the start of the transition from the 'military' to the 'domestic' style in château architecture. Down came the bleak walls and up went the living quarters with their large windows and sweeping staircases. Terraces and gardens were made in the Italian style. The 15th and 16th centuries were the era of the 'Royal Loire', when the kings and queens of France held court here, only two day's ride from Paris, and their followers built châteaux nearby.

Each of the châteaux has its own appeal. Amboise oozes history, and has been restored to the regal appearance it had when it was home to five French kings. Azay-le-Rideau is a thing of beauty, mirrored in a moat that was built for aesthetic reasons, not defensive. The fascinating astrologer's room at Chaumont recalls Catherine de'Medici and her plots to overthrow her rivals, particularly Diane de Poitiers, owner of nearby Chenonceau, arching across the Cher River.

Some châteaux witnessed important events in French history. At Chinon, Jeanne d'Arc convinced Charles VII that she could boot the English out of France (*see pp88–9*). In the equally sombre Langeais, Charles VIII's marriage to Anne of Brittany brought the Bretons under the French flag. Loches may have chilling dungeons, but the beauty of Agnès Sorel, the first

Da Vinci's former home now houses a museum

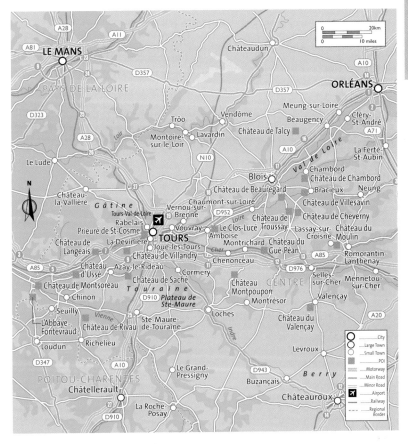

'official' royal mistress, still haunts the castle. The Sleeping Beauty of Ussé is imaginary, the creation of fairy-tale author Charles Perrault, while at Villandry, the main attraction is down-to-earth: the formal gardens.

Not everything is on a grand scale. The valley of Le Loir River has romantic villages. The town of Richelieu was an early example of urban planning. There are shrines to three of France's greatest writers: the poet Pierre de Ronsard, who lived at the priory of St-Cosme en l'Isle François on the outskirts of Tours; the novelist Honoré de Balzac, who wrote at Saché; and Rabelais, who grew up at La Devinière and drank with his friends in Chinon. Then there was artist and inventor Leonardo da Vinci, who lived out his last days at Le Clos-Lucé in Amboise. All this, plus the medieval cathedral city of Tours, ensures plenty of choice for the visitor.

Tours

Motorists on the A10 motorway, speeding past this city of 300,000 people, see modern factories, sprawling suburbs and, very briefly, the River Loire. They miss the Gallo-Roman walls, the medieval stained glass in the Cathedral of St-Gatien, scores of half-timbered and Renaissance buildings and some unusual small museums. All of this lies within a compact city centre full of restaurants, shops and students.

The city became known as Tours, after the Turones, the Gallic tribe who settled on the north bank of the Loire, instead of keeping its Roman name, Caesarodunum (Caesar's Hill). Even so, the Roman site, set between the Loire and Cher rivers, is the base of today's city. Although nothing remains of the amphitheatre, where thousands of spectators once cheered their heroes, portions of brick and stone Gallo-Roman walls still stand by the river and off rue des Ursulines, not far from the cathedral. A separate district, called Châteauneuf (or Martinopolis), stands to the west and dates from the 5th century. The focus here was the early Christian basilica, with the shrine of St Martin, bishop of Tours.

When (in 1461) King Louis XI built his château at Plessis-lès-Tours, 3km west of this basilica, the city prospered

Place Plum in Tours

greatly, becoming known for its silk- and gold-embroidered fabrics. Its mint already produced the official currency, the *denier tournois*. The 16th-century Wars of Religion signalled the end of the glory days and Tours sank into provincialism. By the early 19th century, its population of 20,000 was less than that of Angers or Orléans.

Like many other French cities, Tours was badly damaged during World War II – during the 1960s work began on rebuilding the old city, thanks to the efforts of Jean Royer, the mayor of Tours for 36 years. Yet Tours is no living museum. Balancing the large numbers of professionals who live here is the large population of students attending the university and its famous international language school Institut de Touraine.

'*La douceur de vivre existe toujours*' (Here, the good life still goes on) is how one Tours resident sums up the attractions of the liveliest city on the Loire. It is also known as 'petit Paris' because Victor Laloux, the architect of the Gare d'Orsay in the capital (now the Musée d'Orsay) also designed the railway station in Tours, the town hall and the new basilica of St Martin. Yet despite these grand additions, the development of vibrant squares such as Place Plumereau and the expansion well beyond the banks of the Loire, Tours remains at heart a charming unhurried base from which to explore the region.

Upstairs, downstairs: rue Briçonnet in the Quartier Plumereau

La Basilique Saint-Martin

A strong imagination is required to visualise the enormous 11th-century basilica that once stretched westwards from place de Châteauneuf to the Tour de l'Horloge (Clock Tower). Sacked during the Wars of Religion, it collapsed during the Revolution and was cleared in 1802 to make way for the rue des Halles. Of the original basilica, the rebuilt Tour Charlemagne (the former north transept) remains, decorated with a bas-relief of the saint. St Martin himself is more revered by foreigners than by the French, and visiting pilgrims still come to see the

Ancient tower, modern basilica

shrine in the crypt of the new basilica (1886–1924), built in neo-Byzantine style partly over the site of St Martin's original 5th-century tomb. Around the corner, the Musée St-Martin tells the story of the saint.

Museum: 3 rue Rapin. Tel: 02 47 64 48 87. Open: mid-Mar–mid-Nov Wed–Sun. Admission charge.

Cathédrale Saint-Gatien de Tours

This striking building illustrates the development of the Gothic style, from the mid-13th to the 16th century; to the layman, that means that the architecture ranges from the starkly simple style of the chancel to the flamboyant west front, whose twin towers are crowned with delicate tracery. Equally impressive is the mass of vibrant stained glass and the huge 14th-century rose windows that tower above the transepts.

To the left of the façade are foundation walls dating from the Gallo-Roman period (late 3rd century). It was about this time that St Gatien and St Martin first began preaching the message of Christianity to the people of Tours. St Martin's story is told in the 13th-century stained-glass windows in a chapel off the ambulatory. Beginning at the bottom, these show: St Martin giving half of his cloak to a beggar, then seeing Christ in his cloak; the accident-prone saint being saved by a gold-winged angel from a cheeky devil trying to trip him, then being saved from being crushed by a pine tree. Then, on the right, his body is shown being rowed upstream from the abbey at Candes-Saint-Martin (*see p70*) to Tours, a reference to the legend that St Martin's remains were snatched from Candes by the monks of Tours.

To the south of the choir is the sad tomb of the children of Charles VIII and Anne of Brittany, all of whom died in infancy. Their doll-like effigies are guarded by carved angels. Balzac used the Psalette, or choir school, as the setting for his novel, *Le Curé de Tours*. Protruding from the north flank of the cathedral, the sheltering cloisters form a rectangle where choristers would meet. Above the cloisters, energetic-looking

gargoyles contrast with the delicacy of the Renaissance staircase.
place de la Cathédrale. Open: daily.

Château Royal

All that remains of this 13th-century medieval fortress are two towers. The Tour de Guise, nearest the river, is named after the young Duc de Guise, who was imprisoned here after his father's assassination (*see p57*). Note the height of the window: the boy is said to have jumped from here to freedom. The 18th-century Logis de Mars at the foot of the tower is now used as a contemporary art centre for a wide range of exhibitions.
Tel: 02 47 70 88 46. Open: Tue–Sun.

Église Saint-Julien

This new church was started in 970 after the Vikings destroyed the original, founded by historian-bishop Gregory of Tours in 575. Despite damage during the Wars of Religion, the Revolution and World War II, an 11th-century belfry porch remains. In the chapter house is the **Musée des Vins de Touraine** (Touraine Wine Museum), complete with a huge Renaissance wine press. The cloister houses the **Musée du Compagnonnage** (Trade Guild Museum), displaying hundreds of 'exam' pieces made by apprentices, from satin wedding shoes to a scale model of Milan cathedral (*see p155*).
rue Nationale.
Musée des Vins de Touraine: Tel: 02 47 61 07 93. Open: Wed–Sun, mid-Jun–mid-Sept daily. Musée du Compagnonnage: Tel: 02 47 21 62 20. Open: Wed–Mon mid-Jun–mid-Sept daily. Admission charge for both.

Musée des Beaux-Arts de Tours

The Fine Arts Museum is housed in the 17th-century archbishop's palace; there are fine views of the cathedral. In the Salle de la Régence, locally made red silk brocade recalls Tours' reputation for fine fabrics. The considerable collection of 18th–19th century paintings includes pictures by Boucher,

St-Gatien's Cathedral

Delacroix, Monet, Rembrandt, Rubens, Degas and Mantegna. The peaceful ornamental gardens, dominated by a giant Lebanese cedar are also pleasant to stroll amidst.

18 place François Sicard.
Tel: 02 47 05 68 73.
www.musees.regioncentre.fr. Open:
Wed–Mon. Admission charge.

Musée du Gemmail

A cross between *gemmes* (gems) and *émail* (enamel), this 50-year-old art form faithfully reproduces famous paintings on glass. The best are signed by Picasso, Braque and Rouault. A mini-workshop demonstrates the technique.

Hôtel Raimbault, 7 rue du Mûrier.
Tel: 02 47 61 01 19. Open: Apr–Nov
Tue–Sun Dec–Mar Sat & Sun.
Admission charge.

Quartier Saint-Julien

Rue Colbert is the main street of the characterful St-Julien district, now an area of art galleries and antique shops. Heading eastwards, look out for No. 27, with its carved faces and figures, and at No. 39, where a wrought-iron image of 'La Pucelle Armée' (The Armed Maiden) hangs above a shoe shop; according to legend, Jeanne d'Arc's armour was made in a house on this site. Cross the rue Voltaire. Further on is No. 64 alongside the alley named the Passage du Coeur Navré (Heartbreak Alley), so-called because it was the route to the gallows on place Foire-le-Roi.

Medieval domestic architecture still survives in the place Plumereau

The Wars of Religion (1562–98)

The 16th century brought the creative flowering of the Renaissance from Italy to France. It also saw 36 years of religious conflict between Catholics and Huguenots (the name given to followers of John Calvin (Jean Cauvin), the French Protestant leader).

In 1560, a group of Huguenots tried to petition the young François II for religious freedom – or were they planning his kidnap? When word got out, the court moved from Blois to the greater safety of Amboise. There, the so-called 'Amboise Conspiracy' was foiled and the alleged plotters were caught and either beheaded, drawn and quartered, or hanged from the balcony.

The wars started in earnest after the slaughter of numerous Huguenots in Wassy in 1562; in later years, thousands more died – in massacres in Angers, Orléans and Paris and during the 200-day siege of Sancerre. In revenge, the Huguenots sacked abbeys and churches, such as Beaugency, Marmoutiers and the basilica of St Martin in Tours. At St-Benoît, the fine library was looted, while at Orléans, zealous Huguenots blew up the cathedral tower and most of the nave.

Henri III (1551–89) was caught between the extreme Catholic League, headed by Henri, Duc de Guise, and the Protestants, led by Henri of Navarre. When the Guise faction threatened to usurp the throne, the king took the ultimate sanction: on 23 December 1588 his men murdered the Duc de Guise at Blois. Several months later, King Henri III was himself assassinated by a fanatical Catholic, bringing an end to the Valois line of kings.

In the search for a successor, moderate Catholics supported Henri of Navarre who, in turn, converted to Catholicism (saying 'Paris is well worth a Mass') and in 1589, he was crowned Henri IV. In 1598, he issued the Edict of Nantes, granting the Huguenots equal political rights and limited freedom of worship.

The result was more than 80 years of peace. Then Louis XIV revoked the edict in 1685. He forbade Protestant worship and, although he closed the borders, some 50,000 families, including military leaders, wealthy bankers and merchants, university professors and highly skilled weavers left France forever, taking their money and know-how to more sympathetic countries.

Amboise

This is a delightful town, full of bustle and kept looking smart, thanks to an extensive renovation programme. The rue François I leads past the Hôtel de Ville (Town Hall), with its statue of Louis XI in the courtyard, to the pedestrianised place du Château.

The château

Large parts of the château complex were demolished in the early 19th century, and damaged during World War II but have been restored since. A royal residence between 1434 and 1560, its splendour was due to two monarchs. Charles VIII, born here in 1470, brought the lifestyle of the Renaissance back from Italy and, with his queen, Anne of Brittany, started an ambitious building programme. He died suddenly at the age of 28, after hitting his head on a low doorway. Work continued under François I, who persuaded Leonardo da Vinci to move from his native Italy and live nearby at Clos-

Lucé as chief painter, architect and engineer to the king.

Inside, the most interesting room is the Salle des Etats (the Hall of States), with its double Gothic naves and slender columns. Note the coats of arms of France and Brittany and the ermine, symbol of Queen Anne. Look out, too, for the Conspirators' Balcony: after the attempted 'kidnap' of King François II (*see p57*), the conspirators were hanged from the balustrade or beheaded below. Before entering the Chapelle de Saint-Hubert, stop to admire the carvings above the door. Charles VIII and Queen Anne are shown kneeling either side of the Virgin and Child, while below is a frieze showing St Hubert, patron saint of hunters, stunned by his vision of the Crucified Christ, which appears between the antlers of a stag. The chapel transept houses the tomb believed to hold the body of Leonardo da Vinci.

The Tour des Minimes was built with a 185m- (202yd) long spiral ramp for cavalrymen to ride up to the castle

Azay-le-Rideau Château

from the riverside. Visitors can see only part of it but, in summer, they can walk down to the town through the Tour Heurtault, which has a similar ramp, and fine vault carvings.
Tel: 08 20 20 50 50.
www.chateau-amboise.com.
Open: daily. Admission charge.
Son et Lumière show from late Jun–early Sept.

Amboise's grandiose château complex

Le Clos-Lucé
Leonardo da Vinci (1452–1519) spent the last three years of his life in this red-brick Renaissance manor house, situated just south of the château. The basement now houses a display of 40 models based on his inventions, ranging from tanks and fan-shaped guns to a swing bridge and even a flying machine.

As well as accessing his bedroom, study and the house's communal areas, visitors can stroll through the private parkland attached to the house, which reveals full-scale replicas of his inventions and giant canvasses of his paintings and drawings hung in the trees.
Rue Victor-Hugo. Tel: 02 47 57 00 73.
www.vinci-closluce.com. Open: daily.
Admission charge.

Amboise is 24km (15 miles) east of Tours, on the south bank of the Loire.

Azay-le-Rideau
Like two beauty queens, Azay and Chenonceau compete for the title of 'most beautiful château on water'. Both are described as 'feminine' because they were commissioned by women, but their elegance is typically Renaissance. The turreted towers are for trysts rather than sentry duty, while the machicolations look like a border of crimped pastry. Built on the Indre River, the name comes from Ridel or Rideau d'Azay, a 12th-century knight, but the present château was built by a mayor of Tours, the financier Gilles Berthelot – or rather by his wife, Philippa Lesbahy, who supervised the work.

In 1527, after a scandal, the château was taken over by François I. His emblem, the fire-breathing salamander, is carved above the fireplace in the Chambre du Roi (the King's Chamber) as well as on the front of the building, followed by his wife's symbol, the ermine. Despite the grand staircases the interior is less impressive than the lovely exterior, reflected in its mirror-like moat.
26km (16 miles) southwest of Tours on the D751. Tel: 02 47 45 42 04. Open: daily. Admission charge.
Son et Lumière show: Jul–Aug evenings.

Diane de Poitiers' garden

Chaumont-sur-Loire

The sight of the fortified entrance to this château is worth the 200m (218yd) uphill walk. Cross the drawbridge slowly, playing 'spot the symbol': the volcano (*chaud mont* – hot mountain) is the emblem of the castle. At eye level, the intertwined 'C's refer to owner Charles d'Amboise and his wife, Catherine; the 'D', alternating with a bow, horn and quiver stands for Diane de Poitiers, the favourite of King Henri II (*see p65*).

Like many state-owned châteaux, it is sparsely furnished and you may be content to view the exterior. Standing on the castle terrace it is possible to appreciate the commanding position of this site. For once, the original fort was not built by the legendary Foulques III Nerra (*see p68*), but by his brother-in-law as a defence against him. Today's structure dates mainly from the period 1465 to 1510, though later owners put in large windows and pulled down the north wing to open up the view.

Inside, there is a collection of 18th-century medallion portraits, including one of the bespectacled American inventor, Benjamin Franklin. The Italian artist, JB Nini, worked in a pottery in the stables. More carved symbols decorate the massive fireplace in the dining room, while the floor in the council chamber is covered in 17th-century Italian tiles, put in a century ago. The fine 19th-century landscaped gardens surrounding the château resemble an English country garden and are well worth exploring. *47km (29 miles) east of Tours on the N751. Tel: 02 54 51 26 26. www.chaumontsurloire.info. Open: daily. Admission charge.*

Chenonceau

'*S'il vient à point, me souviendra*' (When it's finished, they'll remember me) reads the inscription over the entrance. Sadly, few do think of Thomas Bohier, the château's early

16th-century owner. Most focus on its feminine mystique. Bohier's wife, Catherine Briçonnet, oversaw the initial building work, which was extended by Diane de Poitiers, mistress of King Henri II and rival of his queen, Catherine de'Medici, who took it over as soon as the king died, forcing Diane to accept Chaumont in return.

Now Chenonceau is one of the top attractions in France. Owned by the Menier family (of chocolate fame), this is a slicker commercial operation than most châteaux and there is a separate waxworks museum explaining the building's history.

Instead of approaching the draw-bridged entrance directly, veer left and circle the sunken Italian garden to get the famous view of the building, with its six-arched entrance bridge across the Cher River; on the right is Catherine de'Medici's garden, surrounded by substantial mature trees. Inside, in the chapel, glass protects the dates scratched into the wall by Henri II's Scots Guards. In the room of Diane de Poitiers, carved 'D's and 'H's are interlinked over the fireplace, ironically beneath a replica portrait of Catherine de'Medici. The 60m long gallery, built across the water, housed wounded soldiers in World War I; the busts of famous personages on the wall are unfortunate additions of the 19th century.

The kitchens set up in two hollow piers of the château comprise a butlery, pantry, larder, cooking area and small harbour through which food was delivered to the château. The rooms above them contain several more reminders of the women of Chenonceau. The Room of the Five Queens bears the coats of arms of five royal spouses, with those of Mary, Queen of Scots above the bed. On the top floor, the Louise de Lorraine Chamber recalls the widow of the assassinated Henri III, who retreated to the château and decorated her room with bone, shovel and skull motifs.

Boat trips on the Cher and musical evenings are attractive extras in July and August.

31km (19 miles) southeast of Tours on the Cher. Tel: 02 47 23 90 07. www.chenonceau.com. Open: daily. Admission charge.

Chenonceau on the River Cher

Chinon

'Chinon, Chinon, Chinon,
Petite ville, grand renom,
Assise sur pierre ancienne
Au haut le bois, au pied la Vienne.'

François Rabelais' verse sums up Chinon well: small town, great renown, sitting on an ancient rock, the forest above, the Vienne below. Henry II of England built the castle, at the hub of his French empire, and he died here in 1189. A decade later, his son Richard the Lionheart died in the Old Town, at the **Hôtel des États-Généraux** on rue Voltaire. Today, this is one of many restored buildings on a street as atmospheric as any in France. Rabelais wrote about the *Caves Painctes* (sic), or Painted Caves, whose drinking club honours the 'Sacred Bottle', while the **Musée Animé du Vin et de la Tonnellerie** (Wine and Cooperage Museum) is aimed at modern wine-lovers. To the right, the rue Jeanne d'Arc is supposed to be the steep route she took up to the château to seek out the Dauphin, the uncrowned Charles VII (*see pp88–9*).

Château

Although a ruin, this castle, currently nearing the end of a major restoration project, still impresses, its curtain wall enclosing an area the size of four playing fields. The entrance to the middle castle is over a moat and under the 14th-century Tour de l'Horloge. Jeanne d'Arc would have heard the

Marie Javelle bell chiming, as it has done regularly since 1349, but only the fireplace stands in what was once the Great Hall, where she picked out the Dauphin despite his disguise. The views of Chinon from the ramparts and the mill tower are superb, and the westerly Fort du Coudray boasts steps leading down past cells (where Knights Templar were imprisoned in 1308) into the bowels of the hill.

Musée du vieux Chinon Hôtel des États-Généraux, rue de Voltaire. Tel: 02 47 93 18 12. www.chinon-histoire.org. Open: daily. Admission charge.

Château: Tel: 02 47 93 13 45. www.fortresse-chinon.fr. Open: daily. Admission charge.

Chinon is 47km (29 miles) southwest of Tours on the D751.

L'Abbaye Fontevraud

Empty but evocative, this once-powerful abbey, the largest of its kind in France, is the final resting place of the early Plantagenet kings and queens of England (*see p39*). The creamy white church is an echoing mausoleum, with just four recumbent effigies in the crypt: Henry II of England (1133–89), his sword on his left; his queen, Eleanor of Aquitaine (1122–1204), holding a Bible in her hands; their son, Richard I, the Lionheart (1157–99); and their daughter-in-law, Isabelle of Angoulême (d.1246). Isabelle's is the only wooden figure; the others are made of painted stone. The hearts of her husband, John I of England (1167–1216), and their son,

Henry III (1207–72), are also buried in the abbey.

Founded in 1099, it housed five separate communities of priests, nuns, lepers, invalids and lay sisters – all under the management of an abbess. Protected by powerful patrons, it also provided a retreat for exiled noblewomen, such as Queen Eleanor.

Use your imagination to visualise the abbey's daily life. The cloister, the largest and finest in France, was not for chatting but for meditating; the chapter house held morning meetings to allocate jobs. The 16th-century murals, depicting the abbess washing the feet of the community on Good Friday, were often updated when a new abbess took over. The only room to be heated was the *chauffoir* or Salle Commune, used for writing and sewing. In the enormous 60m- (196ft) long refectory, nuns would only have sat on one side of the long tables, facing the wall and not each other. Cooking in the stunning Romanesque kitchens was done over one of several side hearths, lighted in pairs depending on the wind direction.

Desecrated by Huguenots in the 16th century and revolutionaries in the 1790s, Fontevraud became a gaol under Napoleon; the last prisoner only left in 1985. Today, it is a cultural centre, with concerts virtually every weekend of the year, usually held in the upper dormitory or the refectory, both noted for fine acoustics. Over the years intensive replanting of the grounds has restored the gardens to their former magnificence.

58km (36 miles) southwest of Tours, 5km south of the Loire. Tel: 02 41 51 71 41. www.abbaye-fontevraud.com. Open: daily. Admission charge.

Royal family: Eleanor of Aquitaine next to her husband, Henry II of England

Ladies of the Loire

Whether peasant, mistress, seductress or queen, these ladies of the Loire made their mark on French history (*see also* Jeanne d'Arc, *pp88–9*).

Eleanor of Aquitaine, twice a queen

Helen of Troy caused a war of 10 years' duration; without Eleanor, the Hundred Years War between England and France would never have happened (*see p39*). Strong, beautiful and wealthy, Eleanor married Prince (later King) Louis VII of France in 1137. After the union was annulled in 1152, she married a younger man, Henri Plantagenet, Comte d'Anjou, bringing one-third of France as her

Agnès Sorel

dowry. Two years later, he was crowned Henry II of England and Eleanor was again queen. She died at Fontevraud in 1204.

Agnès Sorel, royal mistress

Beautiful and intelligent, Agnès was the acknowledged favourite of King Charles VII. They spent time at Loches (*see pp67–8*) where her serene marble effigy is supported by two angels. In life, her easy-going attitude shocked many; two portraits depict her bare-breasted. While some condemned her extravagance, others praised her support for a weak king. Allegedly poisoned, she died, pregnant, in 1450.

Anne of Brittany, Queen of France

Brittany was an independent kingdom until it was absorbed by France at Anne's marriage to Charles VIII in 1491. Anne was then only 15; at 23, she was a widow. Moreover, the nuptial contract dictated that she marry the king's successor, Charles's cousin, Louis XII. The châteaux at Langeais, Amboise and Blois are embellished with her initial 'A', plus her symbol, the ermine. She died in 1514.

Diane de Poitiers and Catherine de'Medici – mistress versus wife

Although 20 years older than Henri II, Diane held him enthralled. She ran the court, brought up the royal

Catherine de'Medici

children, relished her power and loved Chenonceau, presented to her by the king. When he died, Queen Catherine de'Medici took both the power and the château, giving Chaumont to Diane in compensation. For 10 years until her death at Blois in 1589, Catherine ruled France through her three sons, François II, Charles IX and Henri III.

Escadron Volant

Catherine de'Medici's special weapon was the Flying Squad (Escadron Volant), a group of beautiful, blue-blooded Mata Haris who furthered the queen's ambitions by seducing her (male) opponents. At Chenonceau, they enlivened festivities by leaping out from behind bushes, dressed provocatively, to welcome the guests.

Château du Gué-Péan, a modest 'castle'

Le Grand-Pressigny

Located in the castle of this quiet town at the junction of the Aigronne and Claise rivers is the prehistory museum. In Neolithic times, flints shaped here were exported all over Europe. Now the axes and scrapers are under glass, along with fossilised shells and sharks' teeth. The 12th-century, 35m- (115ft) high castle keep and 16th-century Italianate wing dominate, while seven handsome arches in the garden are the sole reminders of a Renaissance gallery.

59km (36 miles) south of Tours, via the N10, D750 and D42.

Musée de la Préhistoire: Tel: 02 47 94 90 20. Open: daily. Admission charge.

Château du Gué-Péan

Gué-Péan is a typical 16th-century château – a country house masquerading as a castle. Even the defensive moat has now dried up. Situated on the edge of the Forest of Choussy, its 'hunting-lodge' description belies the luxury of its Renaissance

interior. The *grand salon* has an awesome fireplace, with carved stone angels and garlands. The art collection contrasts Fragonard and Dali, Guido and Klein, Caravaggio and Carzou. Outside, three towers have the familiar pepper-pot roofs; the fourth is topped by a sterner bell-shaped dome and lantern. Had tabloid newspapers existed in the 16th century, they would have splashed news of the secret wedding here between Mary Tudor of York, sister of the English king, Henry VIII, and Charles Brandon, Duke of Suffolk. The former owner, the Marquis de Keguelin, was a hero of the World War II Resistance.

Monthou-sur-Cher, 50km (31 miles) east of Tours, just north of the N76. Tel: 02 54 71 37 10. Open: telephone to check timings. Admission charge.

Château de Langeais

No fairy-tale château this, but rather a menacing feudal fortress, largely unaltered since its initial construction, whose walls and ramparts are wedged right into the town. In 1886, M. Jacques Siegfried rescued the castle, furnished it with 15th-century beds, tapestries and tables, and gave it to the state in 1904.

The drawbridge of the L-shaped castle was ordered by Louis XI in 1465 to block any attack from the Bretons. That threat evaporated when his son, Charles VIII, married Anne de Bretagne (of Brittany) here in 1491. There are reminders throughout: the initials K (for Karolus, Latin for Charles), A (for Anne), the ermine (Anne's heraldic symbol), and the *fleur de lys* of France. Some of the so-called *mille fleurs* (thousand-flower) tapestries have recognisable daffodils, pinks, violets and cowslips.

Upstairs is a reproduction of a 'noble's bed', the 13th-century precursor to the canopied four-poster, with curtains hung by ropes from the beams. Less inspiring is the recreation of the royal wedding in the Great Hall (Room 8), where 15 wax mannequins

recreate the secret liaison – both Charles and his 15-year-old bride were already betrothed to others. Don't miss the back of the door, which is heavily carved with exotic men-at-arms.

The most atmospheric part of the castle is the 130m (426ft) walk along the ramparts. Luckily the 171 machicolations are covered by planks, but parents should still hold on to children stretching to see the rooftop views.

Behind the château stand the ruins of the oldest surviving stone *donjon* (keep) in France, built to defend the Anjou/Touraine border in 994. *23km (14 miles) southwest of Tours on the N152. Tel: 02 47 96 72 60. www.chateau-de-langeais.com. Open: daily. Admission charge.*

Loches

Set on the Indre River, this handsome town of cobbled streets and slate-roofed, white-stone houses was once a royal residence. In 1429, Jeanne d'Arc hurried to Loches château to persuade

Waxwork version of history, as Brittany is united with France

West Central Loire

the Dauphin to go to Reims for his coronation (*see pp88–9*). Indecisive and glum, Charles only found cheer in Agnès Sorel, the first officially recognised royal mistress (*see p65*). Despite her demure-looking white marble effigy, she knew how to show off her figure, and started a fashion at the French court of dressing in gauze, which did little to hide her shapely breasts. She also posed bare-breasted for Jean Fouquet's famous portrait of her as the Virgin Mary, a copy of which adorns the château. The square, 37m- (121ft) high *donjon* (keep) built by Foulques III Nerra (*see box*) was used as a prison until 1926. The 11th-century keep and 15th-century towers are famous as torture chambers. Back in 1500, the Duke of Milan, locked up for four years in the Martelet Tower, covered the walls in military murals.
43km (27 miles) southeast of Tours on the N143.
Château: Tel: 02 47 59 01 32. www.chateau-loches.fr. Open: daily. Admission charge.

Time stands still in the streets of Loches

FOULQUES III NERRA (987–1040)

The third Comte d'Anjou was a fearsome commander, a jealous husband, a greedy neighbour and an inveterate builder. His castle in Angers was one of a network stretching eastwards along the Loire Valley as far as Montrésor, built to protect his conquered lands.

Montbazon, Montrichard and Loudun illustrate his skill in choosing a site; the ruins at Loches and Langeais show the skill of his masons. He also founded the abbeys at Rançeray and Beaulieu-lès-Loches, no doubt to save his soul after all that conquering and pillaging.

Loudun

Loudun will come as a disappointment for anyone expecting an insight into the 17th-century witch hunt that inspired Aldous Huxley's book *The Devils of Loudun* and Ken Russell's film of 1971. The ruined Tour Carrée, built by Foulques III Nerra in 1040, is the only historic building of any great merit.
72km (44 miles) southwest of Tours on the N147.

Le Lude

The château's fabulous formal gardens lead down to the River Loir. The château dates from the 15th century but over 300 years the fortress gave way to a Renaissance country house. Inside are tapestries and paintings, as well as a large 19th-century library, and the feeling is homely because the de Nicholay family still live here. Underground there is a dimly lit guardroom and a passage from the earlier fortress on the site.

50km (31 miles) northwest of Tours, on the D306 in the Loir valley.
Château: Tel: 02 43 94 60 09.
www.lelude.com. Open: Jul & Aug daily, Apr, May, Jun & Sept Thur–Tue.
Admission charge.

Montoire-sur-le-Loir

Entertainers from a dozen countries enliven this small town during its August folk festival. Montoire's good name was tarnished on 24 October 1940, when Adolf Hitler shook hands here with France's Marshal Pétain, who agreed to collaborate with the Nazi occupation. A fonder memory is of Pierre de Ronsard, the Renaissance poet (see p96) who, in the late 16th century, was the prior of St-Gilles, the Benedictine priory that stands on the river's south bank below the ruined castle. To see the Byzantine-influenced 12th- and 13th-century murals, ask for the key at the tourist office.
45km (28 miles) northeast of Tours in the Loir valley.

Montrésor

The charms of the 'prettiest village in France' may pall on summer weekends when crowds of people come to see the medieval houses with their gardens running down to the Indrois River. The early 16th-century château was restored somewhat fancifully in 1849 by the Polish Count, Xavier Branicki, hence the name, **Polish Museum of Art**. Its curtain wall and towers were built by Foulques III Nerra (see box).
50km (31 miles) southeast of Tours on the D760.
Château (Polish Museum): Tel: 02 47 92 60 04. Open: Apr–end Oct daily.
Admission charge.

West Central Loire

Treasure trove: Montrésor's delights have been discovered but not spoiled

Montrichard

Montrichard is a picturesque town of timber-framed houses clustered beneath the remains of Foulques III Nerra's *donjon* (keep) of 1010, from which there are splendid views, and occasional displays of falconry. The Romanesque church of Sainte-Croix, originally the castle chapel, stands below the keep – it was here that a royal marriage took place in 1476, when Louis XI's daughter, Jeanne, married Louis d'Orléans. The artificial caves and quarries on the north side of the River Cher are used for growing mushrooms and maturing the region's sparkling wines and goat's cheeses.

42km (26 miles) southeast of Tours on the north bank of the Cher. Donjon: Tel: 02 54 32 05 10. Open: Apr–Sept daily. Admission charge.

Château de Montsoreau

Montsoreau, overlooking the confluence of the Loire and the Vienne, served as the setting for the 19th-century novel, *La Dame de Montsoreau*, though the author, Alexander Dumas, rewrote 16th-century history to make a better story. The pleasant little town, hanging over the Loire, makes a convenient base for visitors to tour the region.

Château: Tel: 02 41 67 12 60. www.chateau-montsoreau.com. Open: Apr–Oct daily. Admission charge.

Candes-Saint-Martin

About 1.5km (1 mile) southeast of Montsoreau, this surprisingly large 12th-century monastic church marks the spot where St Martin of Tours (*see p54*) died on 11 November 397. Initially he was buried here but there was considerable rivalry between the monks of Candes-St-Martin and those of Tours over the possession of the saint's remains. In the end, the monks of Tours decided to 'kidnap' the saint. Stained glass in the 12th-century church depicts the saint's body being secretly spirited upstream to Tours as bare trees burst into bloom, even though it was November. The phrase 'St Martin's summer', meaning a freak spell of fine weather, was used by both the French and the English in the old days but has now died out.

Château: Open: daily. Closed: mid-Nov–Feb. Admission charge.

56km (34 miles) southwest of Tours on the south bank of the Loire, 11km (7 miles) from Saumur.

Château Montpoupon

Originally this was the site of a medieval fortress but during the 15th century this Renaissance château was constructed for the Lords of Prie. In the 1920s it was refurbished. The still intact and unusual entrance gatehouse dates from the early 16th century. The same family have lived here for over 200 years. The interior retains a familiar feel and has well-furnished rooms.

The imposing mass of this fortress dominates a wooded valley nearby, which was stocked with game since the family were keen huntsmen. The **Musée du Veneur**, now housed at the château, is dedicated to the huntsman, his passion for horses and thorough knowledge of nature. It includes 25 rooms; there are stables, saddlerooms, blacksmiths and displays of horsedrawn carriages.

Cere la Ronde (near Chenonceaux).
Tel: 02 47 94 21 15.
www.montpoupon.com. Open: daily Jun–Sept. Admission charge.

Prieuré de St-Cosme

The nearby railway line and main road disturb the peace that Pierre de Ronsard, the 'Prince of Poets', would have enjoyed when he was put in charge of this priory in 1565. Then, he worked in his garden, dallied with his 15-year-old mistress (to the scandal of the older monks) and entertained pilgrims on their way south to Santiago de Compostella. He also put off until another day the task of finishing the *Françiade*, an epic poem commissioned by his patron, Charles IX. Today, the gardens are neat and his tomb is shaded by roses. Gregorian chant (played over loudspeakers) drowns out the sound of creaking floorboards in the 12th-century monks' refectory where an elaborate lectern survives. The prior's lodge, open to visitors, was Ronsard's plain stone home.

3km (2 miles) from Tours, in the western suburb of La Riche. Tel: 02 47 37 32 70. Open: daily. Admission charge.

Novel features: Montsoreau is the setting for a popular adventure story

Troglodytes

'Troglodyte: a cave-dweller, especially in pre-historic Western Europe.' What the dictionary doesn't say is that cave-dwellers still exist in the Loire Valley, not living in primitive burrows but in homes with modern conveniences. Warm in winter, cool in summer, protected from the elements and easy to defend, these tunnel homes were a practical choice. Many have been abandoned since or converted into garages or cellars, but a number have also been renovated and patched up to provide unique places to stay: some hotels and chambres d'hôte offer troglodyte rooms and you can even rent a troglogîte for a self-catering holiday underground. The best example of these homes is to be seen alongside the D947 between Montsoreau and Saumur.

Tuffe

The houses and châteaux of the Loire Valley are mainly quarried out of white *tuffe* (tufa), a limestone that

The well-kept exterior of a troglodyte home

Chez moi: yesterday's peasant abodes are today's museums and restaurants

cuts easily and hardens on contact with air. Millions of cubic metres have been extracted from the cliffs that line the Loire, Cher, Indre, Loir and Vienne rivers. The resulting galleries are used to store sparkling wines that need to be turned gently over many months, and also for growing mushrooms, which thrive in the darkness and constant temperature.

Crushed seashells

Falun (oolitic limestone), formed from seashells crushed millions of years ago, is slightly different from tufa. Excavated on farmland south of the Loire, it was once converted to lime for agricultural purposes. Unlike caverns in cliffs, these quarries are hard to spot below the fields of sunflowers but these, too, contrive to be used for homes and storage, with extra galleries dug to create corridors and chambers.

Some are converted into popular, if touristy, restaurants serving hot *fouaces* (bread) baked in wood-fired ovens. One is a museum reflecting everyday life a century ago: another is used for making *pommes tapées* (dried apples); a third is a silkworm farm (*see p150*); and a fourth is a zoo, complete with flamingoes and cheetahs.

Cardinal points: the perfect symmetry of Richelieu's town planning

Richelieu

As the name suggests, this town was created in 1651 by the statesman, Cardinal Richelieu, as a model example of town planning. Richelieu's magnificent palace was dismantled after the Revolution, but the town, with its three triumphal-arched entrances survives. Twenty-eight identical houses, with carriage entrances, line the Grande-Rue; the lower ranks lived behind these.
Richelieu is 62km (38 miles) southwest of Tours on the D757.
www.cc-richelieu.com

Champigny-sur-Veude

Jealous of the magnificence of the Bourbon-Montpensier château (6km north of Richelieu), Cardinal Richelieu bought it, then destroyed it. Luckily, the 16th-century Chapelle St-Louis remains; the colours of the stained glass are still intense today.
Town hall museum: Tel: 02 47 58 10 13. Open: Jul & Aug daily, Sept–Jun Mon & Wed–Fri.

Park: Tel: 02 47 58 10 09. Open: mid-Jun–mid-Sept daily. Admission charge. Chapelle St-Louis: Tel: 02 47 95 73 48. Open: Jul & Aug daily May & Jun Thur–Sun, Sept Wed–Mon. Admission charge.

Château de Saché

Honoré de Balzac (1799–1850) wrote a good number of his 85 novels while staying in this 16th-century château, now furnished as it was in his lifetime. Fans of the 19th-century novelist (*see p96*) come to see his rather plain room in the east wing, with its view of the Indre River and its desk with quill pen and inkwell. He wrote solidly from 5am to 5pm; then read out what he had written to his hosts, the Margonne family. Another local resident, Alexander Calder (1898–1976), famous for his mobiles, lived here for the last 20 years of his life. One of his works remains on the village square.
Saché is 18km (11 miles) southwest of Tours on the Indre River.

Château: Tel: 02 47 26 86 50.
Open: daily. Admission charge.

Sainte-Maure-de-Touraine

The annual cheese fair in June celebrates *le chèvre de Sainte-Maure*, the local goat's cheese identified by the straw running through it. The *fermier* (farm-made) versions are better than the industrial, paper-wrapped *laitier* product.
37km (23 miles) southwest of Tours on the N10.

Seuilly

Rabelais, the burlesque writer (*see p96*), would have laughed to hear experts argue over 'when' and 'where' he was born. Between 1483 and 1494? At 15 rue de la Lamproie in Chinon? Or even in a field, like his legendary hero, Gargantua? La Devinière is now a literary shrine with a small museum of Rabelaisian memorabilia.
52km (32 miles) southwest of Tours. Tel: 02 47 95 91 18. Open: daily. Admission charge.

Trôo

A sleepy artists' colony on the Loir River, Trôo is a showcase for troglodyte homes, many with pretty gardens and terraces (*see pp72–3*). Climb the steep winding paths and steps to Le Puits Qui Parle, the 45m- (147ft) deep 'Talking Well', renowned for its very clear echo. Pilgrims to St Martin's church, dating from the 11th century, nearby, sought a cure for stomach trouble.
Trôo is 54km (33 miles) north of Tours in the Loire Valley.

La Possonnière

This elegant, Renaissance-influenced country mansion (situated 8km southwest of Trôo) is now a shrine to the poet Pierre de Ronsard (*see p96*) who was born here in 1524. Look for the burning roses (*roses ardentes*) on the fireplace in the dining-room, a visual pun (or rebus) on Ronsard's name.
Tel: 02 54 72 40 05. Open: Jul & Aug daily; Apr–Jun & Sept–mid-Nov Fri, Sat, Sun & public holidays. Closed: end Nov–Mar. Admission charge.

The peace of Trôo on Le Loir is especially attractive to artists

Château d'Ussé

Who needs Walt Disney's version of Sleeping Beauty's castle when you can see the real thing? Charles Perrault, the 17th-century fairy-tale author, had this château in mind when he wrote *La Belle au bois dormant* (*The Beauty of the Sleeping Wood*, on which *Sleeping Beauty* is based). Of the castle's ten tableaux depicting the story, the spooky witch in her cave is the best. These tableaux, plus the display of costumes (changed every year to focus on a different century) make this castle more interesting than most for children, while the recently restored Chambre du Roi, the 16th-century ebony-and-ivory-inlaid Italian cabinet or the Flemish tapestries in the long gallery will appeal to the grown-ups. In the park is a small 16th-century chapel, which has been converted into a salon complete with fine furniture and tapestries.

The 'sleeping wood' of Perrault's story, the dense forest of Chinon, stands right behind, offsetting the chimneys, gables, towers and turrets, which were added over the centuries as successive owners 'improved' the building. With the River Indre below, the overall look is charmingly 'romantic'. *40km (25 miles) southwest of Tours, just south of the Loire. Tel: 02 47 95 54 05. www.chateaudusse.fr. Open: Feb–mid-Nov daily. Admission charge.*

Château de Villandry

Villandry is famous for its gardens, which are a 'must-see', even for those who hate gardening. The geometric patterns of the beds and borders look like the doodles of a mathematician, complete with allegorical references to decipher. Don't miss the kitchen garden, where the vegetables are grown and prized as much for their ornamental value as for consumption.

Ussé looks like a fairy-tale castle and is popular with children

Cabbages and kings: Villandry has the world's most elegant vegetable garden

Pink-hearted cabbages were cultivated at Villandry long before they were seen in trendy garden centres.

The gardens, like the château, reflect the Italian influence on 16th-century France. Villandry claims to be the last of the great Renaissance châteaux to be built on the Loire (although it is actually on the south bank of the Cher River). Constructed in 1536 by Jean le Breton, Secretary of State to François I, it was saved in 1906 by Dr Joachim de Carvallo, who restored the castle as well as the gardens. An ardent conserva-tionist, he also founded the Historic Houses Association of France. His Spanish heritage is reflected in the family collection of 17th- and 18th-century paintings, which include works by Goya and Velázquez.

15km (9 miles) west of Tours on the D7, 10km from Azay-le-Rideau. Tel: 02 47 50 02 09. www. chateauvillandry.com. Gardens and château: Open: daily. Admission charge.

Vouvray

Vouvray means wine: it's as simple as that. This village on the Loire, along with its neighbours, Rochecorbon and Parçay-Meslay, produce fine white wines, still and sparkling, dry, medium and sweet. The vines grow on the plateau above; the bottles fill endless galleries in the cliffs below. Visit these and taste the wines at well-known makers such as Marc Brédif, where a circular tasting room has been hollowed out, deep within the rock. *10km (6 miles) east of Tours on the north bank of the Loire.*

Walk: old Tours

The Quartier Plumereau, the city's old quarter, is full of cafés, students and delightfully carved hôtels (mansions) of timber and stone. It has now been restored, thanks to a 35-year renovation programme.

Allow 1 hour.

Start in place du Grand Marché by the tourist information board. Walk north up rue Bretonneau.

1 Rue Bretonneau

The Hôtel des Seigneurs d'Ussé, at no 22, is 15th-century Gothic, though it now houses a Moroccan restaurant. Opposite, the Hôtel Poulet-Grellay recalls the Renaissance, but was built in the 19th century. A plaque on no 35 records the birthplace of the French Communist Party at the Congress of Tours in 1920. Consider a detour up rue du Mûrier to visit the Musée du Gemmial, inside the vine-covered Hôtel Raimbault.
Return to rue Bretonneau; turn right, then right on to rue des Cerisiers.

2 Rue des Cerisiers

The sisters of the famous novelist Honoré de Balzac were educated at no 7, which used to be a 19th-century ladies' academy. Turning right on to rue Briçonnet, the handsome Hôtel des Cordeliers at no 16 is also known as Tristan's House. Try spotting the frog among the carvings above the windows; you will need binoculars to see the detail of the statue at the pinnacle of the Flemish-style gable. Built by Pierre Dupui in 1498, a witty anagram of his name in the interior courtyard reads 'Prie Dieu Pur'. The building is also famed for its spiral staircase.
Continue to place Plumereau.

3 Place Plumereau

The heart of Old Tours, once the hat market, bustles with as many locals as tourists, attracted by the art galleries, boutiques and cafés. Spend a few moments taking in the mixture of architectural styles, as 15th-century timber-frame buildings alternate with later stone buildings. You may have to wait to secure a table in the square, but the cafés, crêperies and bars here are ideal places to watch the world go by.
Turn left (east) along rue du Commerce.

4 Place Saint-Pierre-le-Puellier

Excavations at this pretty square, upon which a Renaissance cloister once stood, have revealed a Gallo-Roman cemetery.

Continue left (east) along rue du Commerce.

5 Rue du Commerce

Here, garish restaurants clash with handsome houses, particularly nos 106–110, with their tall 18th-century windows and balconies. Dip left into rue Paul-Louis Courier. Finely carved heads mark no 17, where the Florentine sculptor, Giovanni Giusti (Jean Juste) lived from 1504. Jeanne d'Arc stayed at no 15 in 1429. The Hôtel Binet, no 10, is an outstanding 15th-century mansion with a wooden gallery above the inner courtyard, reached by spiral staircases.

Return to rue du Commerce; turn left, then right on rue du Président Merville (past the Museum of Natural History), then right again on to rue de la Monnaie.

6 Rue de la Monnaie

The Hôtel de la Monnaie, at no 7, was a mint, producing *sols*, *deniers* and golden *louis* coins from the 13th century until it closed in 1772.

Continue towards place Plumereau. Turn left on to the rue du Change.

7 Rue du Change

On the corner is a wonderful twin-gabled 15th-century house decorated with a carving of the Nativity. At the bottom of the street is the tall, ivy-clad tower of the Briçonnet-Berthelot house, home of the first mayor of Tours, Jean Briçonnet.

Turn left on to place de Châteauneuf.

8 Place de Châteauneuf

The Logis des Ducs de Touraine was the private mansion of the Dukes of Touraine back in the 15th and 16th centuries.

Bear right, on to rue des Halles.

9 Rue des Halles

This street cuts right through the site of the Basilica of St-Martin, pulled down 200 years ago. All that remains are the Tour Charlemagne on the right and, opposite, the tomb of St Martin in the crypt of the 19th-century basilica, plus the Tour de l'Horloge (clock tower) further down the street.

Continue past the clock tower and turn right to return to place du Grand Marché.

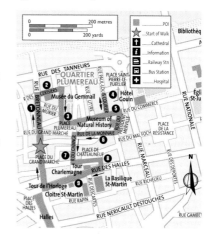

Tour: the Indre

A tranquil river, with picnic sites around every bend in the adjacent road, the Indre has long been at the crossroads of history. This drive goes from Cormery to Buzançais, through pretty countryside with plenty of farms but few tourists.

Allow half a day for the 75km (46-mile) journey, longer if you decide to stop and explore.

Start in Cormery.

1 Cormery

The 50m-high tower of St-Paul is just one indication of the grandeur of the Benedictine monastery founded here in 791. Remnants of the Romanesque cloisters, refectory and chapel still stand in the town. Today, Cormery is more renowned for its macaroons.
Take the D17 to Chambourg.

2 Chambourg-sur-Indre

The road on the north bank is quiet, with the sleepy villages of Courçay, Reignac and Azay.

At Chambourg, cross the bridges to the south bank of the Indre, following the D94 and then the D25 to Beaulieu-les-Loches.

3 Beaulieu-les-Loches

This looks like an extension of Loches on the opposite bank, but Beaulieu's religious community constantly battled for power with the royal court across the river. Foulques III Nerra, the 11th-century warlord, founded the abbey (now in ruins) where he was later buried.
Staying on the north side of the Indre, follow the D92, then the D28, then cross the bridge into Châtillon.

French soldiers tunnelled to victory at Palluau-sur-Indre

4 Châtillon-sur-Indre

Built on a spur of chalk overlooking the river and its peaceful fields, this medieval village of narrow stone streets is full of history. The tourist office has a useful pamphlet mapping out a walk past the 16th-century Maison Henri III with its fine entrance, and the market square with its panoramic view. The 12th-century church has a portal with carvings of Adam and Eve being chased from Eden, plus dancing donkeys, beasts and mythical creatures. The 13th-century château boasts a massive keep, a legacy of Henry II of England.

Cross the bridge to the north bank of the Indre again and pick up the D28 to Palluau.

5 Palluau-sur-Indre

This village has a special place in Canadian history since Louis de Buade (1620–98), Comte de Frontenac and owner of the impressive castle, was made governor of the French possessions in North America in 1672. He took with him Jean-Baptiste Franquelin, another local, who mapped out the territory of Nouvelle-France (New France), which then extended from Canada to the Gulf of Mexico. The Philippe-Auguste Tower commemorates the French king who besieged and defeated Richard the Lionheart here in 1188. English survival depended on a well 108m deep, so when the French tunnelled into the hillside they cut the well-rope. With no water supply, the English were forced to surrender.

Leave Palluau on the D15e; then take the D64 to Buzançais.

6 Buzançais

This quiet market town, today known for its porcelain, has been fought over many times and, as recently as 1846, the peasants revolted against a tax on wheat.

Return to the Loire via the fast but busy N143, along the south bank of the Indre.

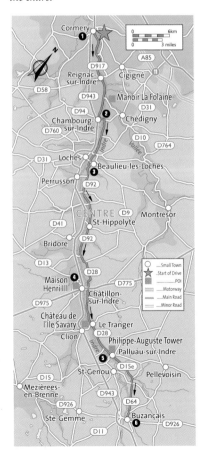

Tour: the Loir

Not to be confused with La Loire, this smaller river wanders past small towns and villages plus vineyards and fields of sunflowers. The poet Pierre de Ronsard (1524–85) was born and lived on its banks. The route follows a 40km (25-mile) stretch between Château-du-Loir and Lavardin.

Allow at least half a day.

1 Château-du-Loir

The keep that gave its name to the village is now a ruin, but the 13th-century church of St-Guingalois, where Ronsard once worshipped, contains fine sculpture in wood and terracotta.
Take the N138 to Coëmont and turn left on to the D64. The road, squeezed between the limestone cliff and the railway line, follows the north bank.

2 Vouvray-sur-Loir

Many wine cellars are open to the public, dug out of the cliffs.

Follow the D64 towards Chahaignes. After Le Port Gautier, turn right for Marçon, crossing the railway bridge.

3 Marçon

The large lake on the left is part of a leisure park offering riding, fishing, sailing and tennis. Marçon itself has a fine, oblong square lined with lime trees. Old houses have been tastefully restored and the shops sell a good range of locally produced wines.
Turn left on to the D305 towards La Chartre. The river is now on your left.

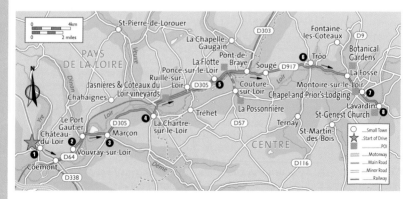

La Chartre is a popular stop for fans of good food and motor-racing

4 La Chartre-sur-le-Loir

This is a classic small French town, with a main square ringed by tempting food and wine shops. The ivy-clad Hôtel de France attracts motor-racing teams for the Le Mans 24-hour race and fans come to see the signed photos in the bar.

Leave by one of the three bridges over the Loir, staying on the D305 for Ruillé and passing through the Jasnières and Côteaux du Loir vineyards where several growers offer dégustations *(tastings).*

5 Poncé-sur-le-Loir

Stop here to see the crafts centre housed in the 18th-century buildings of the former Paillard paper mill. Watch artisans at work, or try throwing a pot on a wheel. The 16th-century château opposite has a remarkable staircase whose ceiling is carved with allegorical subjects, and a dovecote that once housed 1,800 pigeons.

Continue on D305. An optional detour is south on the D57 to La Possonnière,

Ronsard's birthplace (see p75). Otherwise continue through Pont-de-Braye to Trôo.

6 Trôo

The homes of Trôo's troglodyte community can be visited daily between mid-July and mid-August (*see p75*).

Follow the D917 to Montoire. Garden lovers might detour to the right to see the botanical gardens at La Fosse.

7 Montoire-sur-le-Loir

Visit the chapel and prior's lodging where Ronsard spent his last years (*see p69*). The chapel has outstanding Romanesque frescoes.

Continue on the D917 to Lavardin.

8 Lavardin

One of France's most atmospheric villages, Lavardin is dominated by its ruined 12th-century castle. The church of St-Genest has impressive 13th-century frescoes of the *Passion* and *Christ in Majesty*.

East Central Loire

The capital of the Centre-Val-de-Loire administrative region is Orléans, the city relieved by Jeanne d'Arc in 1429, an event still celebrated annually with grand parades in May. Blois, however, claims to have been the capital of France under King Louis XII, who was born in the city in 1462. Today, it is one of the Loire's most attractive cities, with an extensive pedestrian area in the old quarter, a grand town hall and a château that looks like a mini-city in its own right.

Châteaux

The best-known château in this region, is Chambord, the world's largest hunting lodge, with its ingenious double staircase. Other, less famous castles have developed themes to attract visitors: Chamerolles concentrates on perfume, while La Ferté-St-Aubin offers cookery demonstrations. At Sully, a 20-year project is under way to restore the home of its 17th-century duke, one of France's most able ministers.

Talcy was the home of two women, generations apart, who inspired great poetry, while the portrait gallery of Beauregard is a 'who's who' of France in the 14th to 17th centuries. Cheverny, dedicated to hunting, is very much a family home.

Royal Blois: a former capital of France with a fine château, museums and cathedral

See pp110–11 for walk route

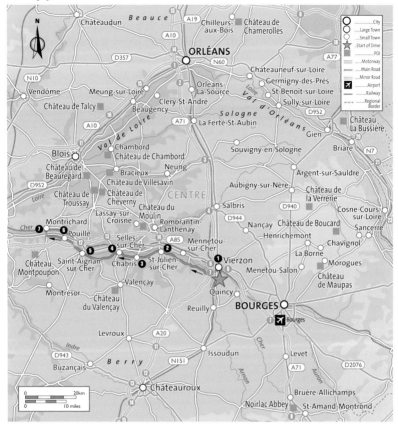

Churches and abbeys

Take in the grandeur of Orléans cathedral and the little-visited Germigny-des-Prés, modestly hiding a 1,200-year-old apsidal mosaic. La Trinité Church in Vendôme is a masterpiece of flamboyant Gothic and the church at Cléry-St-André has the skulls of a French king and queen. Finally, pay tribute to St Benedict, founder of western monasticism, whose remains are buried at St-Benoît-sur-Loire.

Food and wine

The region has produced such chefs as the great Marie-Antoine Carême, 19th-century author of *La Cuisine française*, who worked his magic in the kitchens at Valençay, and the Tatin sisters who, in rescuing an apple pie that had 'gone wrong', invented the Tarte Tatin. Among wines, those of Quincy and Reuilly should be better known than they are, and it is a short step to Sancerre, with its characteristically dry white wines.

Orléans

Orléans is famous for La Pucelle d'Orléans, the Maid of Orléans, Jeanne d'Arc (Joan of Arc). Not surprisingly, her story has sparked a local mini-industry, culminating in the annual May re-enactment of her entrance into the besieged city in 1429. Orléans has always been important as a trading post. Goods from as far south as the Massif Central, and from as far west as Nantes, were brought here by water, then transferred to carts for the onward journey to Paris.

The city's strategic location, and its commerce, have made it a prize fought over in wars throughout French history. The new bridge across the Loire and the city's north–south tramway system, both of which opened in 2000, symbolise the dynamism of Orléans. The east–west tramline is set to open in 2012.

During the 16th-century Wars of Religion, the cathedral was one of the casualties. At the end of the 19th century, following bombardment during the Franco-Prussian War of 1870–71, the Parisian-style boulevard, the rue de la République, was built. Unfortunately, the post-World War II reconstruction is not so handsome.

Although not the largest city in the Centre-Val-de-Loire, Orléans is the regional capital. It had an ancient university, whose students included Rabelais and Jean Calvin (John Calvin), founder of Calvinism, but this closed in 1793 when enrolment had fallen to only one student. The modern university is located 8km away, at Orléans-la-Source. This, plus the fact that Orléans is only 130km (80 miles) from Paris, close enough for a daily commute on the TGV, means that the city lacks the liveliness of, say Tours.

Having said that, the city has some delightful old buildings and streets. The area around the medieval rue de Bourgogne is criss-crossed by *venelles* (alleys), while the rue d'Escures is lined with decorated 16th- and 17th-century mansions, most now occupied by banks. Tucked away in the rue de Notre-Dame de la Recouvrance is the Hôtel Toutin, where King François I rendezvoused with his mistress; his smirking statue sits in the courtyard. The spacious place du Martroi, with its mounted statue of Jeanne d'Arc, is faced by the elegant 18th-century Chancellerie. On the statue's pink granite plinth is a bas-relief depiction of Jeanne D'Arc defending the city. Most characteristic of all, perhaps, is the approach to the cathedral along a broad street named, of course, rue Jeanne d'Arc.

Cathedral of Sainte-Croix

Most cathedrals of the Loire form part of an atmospheric old quarter. This one stands on an open square, looking out on traffic and skateboarders who whizz along the broad terraces. Begun in 1287, it was largely destroyed by Protestants in 1568 but Henri IV repaid the loyalty of the town by promising to repair the damage. Rebuilding, in

(*Cont. on p90*)

Stone tiaras top the towers of Sainte-Croix Cathedral

The Maid of Orléans

Born around 1412 in a village on the border of eastern France, it is here in the Loire Valley that Jeanne d'Arc celebrated her greatest victories during the Hundred Years War against the English.

On God's Command

Jeanne had been having 'visions', in which God sent her divine messages, from the age of 12. It was in response to one of these heavenly messages, which told her to drive the English out of France, that the virgin-warrior went to the aid of the Dauphin, Charles.

It was 1428. The English were preparing to besiege Orléans, thereby gaining control of the Loire Valley. The situation was critical.

A statue of St Joan of Arc

At this stage Charles was in a hopeless position with almost no funds and only a motley collection of foreign mercenaries and local feudal forces as an army.

Jeanne managed to persuade Lord Baudricourt, the garrison commander, to grant her permission to meet Charles. Aged just 17, she set off with a band of six soldiers to see the Dauphin at Chinon, a journey that involved walking 600km (372 miles) through some very dangerous territory. Since a woman risked being raped if captured, she was clothed as a man. Throughout her campaigns she remained in men's clothing for safety and modesty's sake. She was nicknamed 'La Pucelle' (the Maiden or Virgin) since she vowed to remain a virgin 'for as long as it pleases God'.

Persuading the Dauphin

When he heard of her mission, the 26-year-old monarch disguised himself and mingled with his courtiers to test Jeanne. Recognising him at once she persuaded him to march to Orléans, gathering an army as he went, and halting only at Blois for the bishop's blessing.

However, Charles first wanted her beliefs to be examined by

theologians.It was only after three weeks of questioning in Poitiers that Jeanne was finally accepted and given titular command of an army.

The Siege of Orléans

She joined her troops at Blois and the army moved out to arrive between 29 April and 4 May at the now English occupied city of Orléans. Jeanne wanted to attack at once but the military leaders counselled otherwise. So she entered the city by herself, via the eastern Burgundy Gate. On 6 May she led her troops in an impromptu attack, forcing the English to retreat and abandon the city by moving their army to Meung-sur-Loire.

Next, Joan led the French army to drive the enemy from the Loire Valley and then watched as Charles VII was crowed at Reims on 17 July 1429.

Yet the king offered no help when she was betrayed by the Burgundians, tried by French bishops and burnt at the stake by the English. That was in 1431.

It was not until 1920 that Jeanne d'Arc was canonised and declared the patron saint of France.

The Fêtes de Jeanne d'Arc

For over 500 years, from 26 April to 8 May, the Fêtes de Jeanne d'Arc in Orléans has celebrated Jeanne 'for her glory', not, as in Rouen, 'for her martyrdom'. A schoolgirl is chosen to play the role of La Pucelle. Mounted

Orléans Cathedral – stained-glass window showing Jeanne leading her troops

on a horse and dressed in armour, she enters the city through a (temporarily) reconstructed Burgundy Gate. Over the next nine days, there are parades through the city, cathedral services, civic ceremonies and fireworks.

LA MAISON DE JEANNE D'ARC

This is a replica of the home of Jacques Boucher, with whom Jeanne stayed on 29 April, 1429. Less a museum, more a 'maison des souvenirs' (house of memories), its displays explain the sequence of events leading to the raising of the siege of Orléans. A short 'mini Son et Lumière', using a model of the city, is offered in several languages.
3 place de Gaulle. Tel: 02 38 52 99 89.
Open: May–end-Oct 10am–noon & 2–6pm, rest of year 1.30–6pm. Closed: Mon. Admission charge.

neo-Gothic style, took more than 250 years. Blue sky can be seen through the filigree stonework that crowns the two towers. Inside, ten stained-glass windows tell Jeanne d'Arc's story, from her first vision of St Michael, clad in golden armour, to her death at the stake. On the north side is the tomb of Cardinal Touchet, Bishop of Orléans, whose kneeling effigy looks up to Jeanne's statue. His efforts led to her canonisation in 1920.
Tel: 02 38 24 05 05. Open: daily.

Hôtel Cabu

Heavily restored, this Renaissance mansion houses the Historical Museum. Pride of place is given to a horde of Gallo-Roman bronzes, including sculptures of a horse and a wild boar, found nearby at Neuvy-en-Sullias in 1861. Upstairs are fine medieval sculptures and sections devoted to local ceramics, clocks, goldwork and folklore.

Orléans' neo-Gothic cathedral

place Abbé Desnoyers. Tel: 02 38 79 25 60. Open: Oct–Apr Wed, Sat & Sun afternoons, May, Jun & Sept Tue–Sun afternoons only, Jul & Aug Tue–Sun morning & afternoon. Admission charge.

Hôtel Groslot

The sumptuous 16th-century Hôtel Groslot, guarded by an elegant bronze statute of Jeanne d'Arc, once served as the town hall. Built out of diamond-patterned red and black brick, this grand residence once housed French kings. In 1560 the sickly François II fell ill and died here.

A large canvas depicting the death scene hangs in the ornate King's Room, where marriages now take place.
place de l'Etape. Tel: 02 38 79 22 30. Open: daily, except Sat morning. Free admission.

Musée des Beaux-Arts

The strength of this collection, one of the finest in France, is the work of 16th- and 17th-century artists of the Italian, French and Dutch schools, including paintings by Matteo di Giovanni, Tintoretto and Ruysdaal. Several paintings rescued from Cardinal Richelieu's palace have a room to themselves. In the basement, a small modern collection surrounds a room dedicated to Max Jacob, the poet and artist who lived nearby at Saint-Benoît-sur-Loire. A work called *Visions of War* (1940) is a chilling premonition of his own death in a Nazi concentration camp.

The winding staircase at Blois

29km (18 miles) southwest of Orléans.
Château: 2 place Dunois.
Tel: 02 38 44 55 23. Open: Wed–Mon.
Admission charge.

Château de Beauregard

Confused by French history? Head for Beauregard's remarkable portrait gallery with its painted beams, Delft floor tiles, painted panelling and 327 faces ranged in three tiers along the walls. All of the Valois and early Bourbon kings are here, plus the VIPs of their time. The Cabinet des Grelots is a delightful study, panelled in gilded oak and covered in paintings and carvings of *grelots* (bells) from the coat of arms of the 16th-century owner, Jean du Thiers, who turned an old hunting lodge into this elegant château on the Beuvron River.

65km (40 miles) southwest of Orléans,
6km (4 miles) south of Blois. Tel: 02 54
70 40 05. www.beauregard-loire.com.
Open: Easter–Sept daily Oct–Dec &
Feb–Easter Thur–Tue. Admission charge.

Blois

Once the capital of France and famous for its château, Blois is a thoroughly likeable town, run for many years by Jack Lang, the charismatic mayor who went on to become the French Minister of Culture. Stop at the tourist office in the grounds of the château to pick up tour leaflets, and wear comfortable shoes for walking on the cobbles and climbing the hills and stone steps, especially in the medieval Puits-Châtel quarter.

rue Paul-Belmondo, place Ste-Croix.
Tel: 02 38 79 21 55. Open: Tue–Sat.
Admission charge.

Beaugency

Much restored, this is now one of the most attractive towns in the region. Locals are nicknamed *les chats* (the cats) because the ancient bridge was supposedly built by the devil in exchange for the soul of the first creature to cross it – crafty locals ensured that this was a cat. The 'Devil's Bridge' is the only river crossing for many kilometres up- or downstream, and its strategic importance is emphasised by the still-impressive Tour de César, the ruined 11th-century keep, built to protect the bridge. Across the road is the fine Romanesque abbey church of Notre-Dame, while the **Château Dunois**, containing a museum of local life (Musée Régional de l'Orléanais), stands to the north.

Château

The château is fascinating for its architecture and tales of love and intrigue. The oldest room is the 13th-century Salle des États (Hall of States), simply designed but heavily decorated. Two centuries later, the St-Calais chapel was built after poet-duke Charles d'Orléans returned from 25 years in the Tower of London. His son, Louis, unexpectedly became King Louis XII in 1498. His additions include the brick-and-stone east wing and the charming pavilion in the gardens (now the tourist office). Next came François I, whose wing has an elaborate, semi-open staircase facing the courtyard and, facing the town, the extraordinary Façade des Loges, whose tiers of galleries look like theatre boxes.

Blois is also known for the assassination in 1598 of the Duc de Guise, the ultra-Catholic, ultra-powerful rival of Henri III during the Wars of Religion (see p57). The deed was done in the Chambre du Roi (King's Room), with Henri supposedly listening behind the small door. Within a year Henri himself had been murdered. The study of his mother, Catherine de'Medici, is heavily decorated; some of the 200 panels hide secret drawers and cupboards, allegedly for storing her poisons.

The château houses the Musée des Beaux-Arts, with collections covering archaeology and local history, sculpture, 16th–17th century portraits and painting and also locks and keys.

Opposite the château is the **Maison de Magie**, which is devoted to mechanical wizard, inventor and magician, Robert-Houdin. Enter into this magical world and discover illusions from throughout the ages. Particularly fascinating is the Hallucinoscope that takes you on a voyage 'twenty thousand leagues under the sea' with Jules Verne. A great place for children. The Son et Lumière in summer is one of the Loire Valley's best.
Tel: 02 54 90 33 33.
www.chateaudeblois.fr. Open: daily.
Maison de Magie: Tel: 02 54 55 26 26.
www.maisondelamagie.fr. Open: daily.
Closed: some Mon in low season, phone to check. Admission charge.
Son et Lumière shows: Jun–Sept
(tel: 02 54 78 72 76 for details).
Admission charge.

59km (36 miles) southwest of Orléans on the north bank of the Loire.

Chambord

Chambord is the largest of all the Loire châteaux. Some 1,800 men worked on the decoration of the 440 rooms, putting in 365 fireplaces and 83 staircases. Marshes were drained and the Cosson River rerouted. Despite all this, there was no proper kitchen and only limited toilets, for this was no more than a hunting lodge, a pleasure palace and a stage for displaying the wealth of François I. When Charles V of Spain visited in 1539, he was suitably stunned by the gilded roof, and by the fine furniture and tapestries brought in just for his visit.

Today the interior is disappointingly empty, except for the château's signature feature, the double-helix staircase conceived by Leonardo da Vinci where visitors walk up and down in sight of one another, yet never meet. Hundreds of fire-breathing salamanders and letter 'F's, the emblems of the king, decorate the palace, particularly in the *studiolo*, or little study.

Audio-visual and model displays do their best to explain a grandeur that is impossible to recreate.

The wall surrounding the estate is some 33km (20 miles) long, the same length as the *périphérique* (ring road) that surrounds Paris; the forest that it encloses, a national hunt reserve, is alive with wild boar and deer. The grounds are freely open to the public. Enjoy Chambord at dawn or dusk, when mist emphasises the tiara-like roof enrichments, all intricately carved and overlaid with ornate slates in imitation marble. Quite unique.

Near Bracieux, 52km (32 miles) southwest of Orléans off the D951, south of the Loire. Tel: 02 54 50 40 00. www.chambord.org. Open: daily. Son et Lumière: end Jun–Aug. Admission charge.

Château de Chamerolles

Beautifully restored, the château at Chamerolles is now dedicated to sweet smells, with explanations of the manufacture and distillation of perfume and a collection of historic scent bottles. Even the gardens are planted with aromatic herbs, spices and flowers.

At Chilleurs-aux-Bois, 30km (18 miles) northeast of Orléans off the N152. Tel: 02 38 39 84 66. Open: daily except Tue. Admission charge.

The royal hunting lodge at Chambord is the largest of the Loire châteaux

Walk: old Orléans

There's still a very real sense of grandeur in old Orléans, the quarter defined by the Loire, the cathedral and Place du Martroi. Badly damaged during World War II, it has been carefully reconstructed. This short stroll provides a good introduction and insights into the past of France's former capital by exploring this area.

Allow 45 minutes.

Start facing the main entrance of Ste-Croix Cathedral. Turn right and enter the old quarter along rue Parisie. Take the second turning on the right.

1 Rue de Bourgogne

This was once the main Roman street. The circular church on the right, covered with carved angels' faces, dates from 1837. Number 261 is a fine medieval mix of brick, timber and stone, while no 264 is now a British-style pub. Spot the modern *trompe l'oeil* above the intersection with rue de la Cholerie.

Turn right on to rue Ste-Catherine.

2 Hôtel des Créneaux

This 15th-century mansion was, until 1790, the town hall. The façade dates from the 16th century and combines Gothic and Renaissance styles. The belfry next door dates from 1445.

Turn left on to rue Isabelle Romée

3 Place Abbé Desnoyers

Behind the belfry on this new square is the stone façade of the Renaissance Maison de la Pomme, boasting carved faces and the apple after which it is named. Across the square, the house built by Philippe Cabu in 1548 was nicknamed the Maison de Diane de Poitiers after the mistress of Henri II stayed here. Now it houses the Historical Museum (*see p90*).

Turn left on to rue Royale and admire the highly decorated Hôtel Euverte Hatte, now the Charles Péguy Cultural Centre. Turn right on to rue du Tabour.

4 Maison de Jeanne d'Arc

Though the maison looks medieval, it is a careful copy of Jacques Boucher's home. Next door, the Maison de la Porte Renard is genuinely 15th-century. An arch on the right leads to the garden surrounding the Pavillon Colas des Francs, a 16th-century counting-house.

Cross place du Général de Gaulle. Turn left on to rue des Minimes.

5 Couvent des Minimes

Look down the Passage du Chanoine Chenesseau for glimpses of the 17th-century arches of the convent. The cloister arcades are decorated in a simple white stone pattern typical of the 17th century. The church now houses the Archives Museum.
Retrace your steps, then turn left on to rue d'Illiers into the city's main square.

6 Place du Martroi

Follow the story of Jeanne d'Arc as carved on the base of her 19th-century statue. To the right, the handsome Chancellerie de Commerce is where the Duc d'Orléans kept his paperwork.
Leave the square on the rue d'Escures.

7 Église Saint-Pierre du Martroi

This is the city's only brick church. The Pavillons d'Escures on the left is a fine 17th-century town-house development, inspired by the mayor, Pierre Fougeu d'Escures. The porch of the Groslot garden is from the Saint-Jacques pilgrims's chapel that once stood by the Loire.
At the end of rue d' Escures, turn right on to the place de l'Étape.

8 Hôtel Groslot

Built for the city bailiff in 1555, this building was given a Gothic Revival facelift 300 years later. A greenish-bronze statue of Jeanne d'Arc stands in front of the hôtel, which served as the town hall from 1790 to 1982.

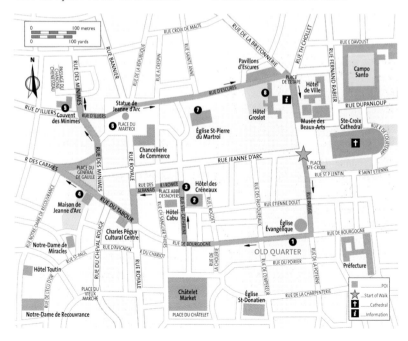

Writers of the Loire

For centuries, the Loire Valley has attracted writers. English diarist John Evelyn went to Tours to perfect his French, Beaumarchais (who wrote *The Barber of Seville*) lived in Vouvray, while Rousseau stayed in Chenonceau and Voltaire in Sully.

François Villon (1431–89)

Born François de Montcorbier, Villon is best remembered for his irreverent and humorous writing, though his *Epitaphe Villon* is a serious plea for the compassionate treatment of criminals; he himself was convicted of manslaughter in 1455 and was imprisoned in Meung-sur-Loire (*see p101*).

François Rabelais (1494–1553)

First a monk, then a doctor, Rabelais will always be remembered for his brilliant satirical books, *Gargantua* (1534) and *Pantagruel* (1532), in which he entertained the middle classes but shocked theologians by treating serious ideas within an often irreverent context.

Pierre de Ronsard (1524–85)

Born in La Possonnière near Vendôme on the Loir, Ronsard was plagued by deafness, so he left diplomatic life and settled at St-Cosme, near Tours, where he penned his sonnets and odes, which, in their time, were not well received. Now his works, especially his love poems, are appreciated for their freshness and lyricism.

Honoré de Balzac (1799–1850)

Balzac was the chief exponent of the realistic novel. Many were scathing insights into the hypocrisy of the French society of his time. He grew up in Tours and Vendôme, and frequently returned to Saché, near Chinon, to write and recharge his batteries after the excesses of Parisian life.

Balzac, social commentator

Max Jacob (1876–1944)
Poet, artist and friend of Picasso, Jacob left the bohemian life of Montmartre for the solitude of St-Benoît-sur-Loire. A Jewish convert to Catholicism, he was deported by the Nazis and died in a concentration camp before his friends could rescue him.

Maurice Genevoix (1890–1980)
Elected to the Academie Française in 1946, this prolific writer's best-known novel is *Raboliot*, the tale of a Sologne poacher for which he won the prestigious *Prix Goncourt* in 1925. He lived at St-Denis-de-l'Hôtel.

Jules Verne (1828–1905)
Growing up in Nantes, Jules Verne's appetite for adventure, inspired by the busy quays, later gave rise to the new genre of science fiction, in such gripping works as *Twenty Thousand Leagues Under the Sea* (1865) and *Around the World in Eighty Days* (1873).

Henri Alain-Fournier (1886–1914)
See p126.

Illustration from Jules Verne's *Twenty Thousand Leagues Under the Sea*

Châteaudun

The citizens of Châteaudun were collectively awarded the Légion d'honneur (France's highest award) after 900 defenders held out against a Prussian force of 12,000 in 1870. For centuries, this rocky outcrop above the Loir has been a strategic stronghold, its daunting 45m- (147ft) high, 12th-century keep one of the first to be built with rounded walls. Next to it, the Ste-Chapelle boasts 12 life-sized, painted statues, carved in the mid-15th century: St Agnes is portrayed with a lamb and St Apollonia, patron saint of surgeons, holds a tooth and forceps. In the château, the Dunois Wing is named after the Comte who was one of Jeanne d'Arc's most faithful comrades-in-arms. Gothic, gaunt and bare (without furniture, but hung with tapestries), this contrasts with the richly decorated Renaissance Longueville wing.
51km (31 miles) northwest of Orléans on the D955. Château: Tel: 02 37 94 02 90. Open: daily. Admission charge.

The Cheverny clock will tell you the date, day, month and . . . time

Châteauneuf-sur-Loire

This affluent-looking dormitory town, just east of Orléans, has suffered twice: the French Revolution saw the destruction of its mini-version of Versailles, and World War II brought aerial bombing. Two attractions survived: in the château gardens, designed by Le Nôtre, the rhododendrons thrive, while in the old guardroom of the château the **Loire Nautical Museum** records the river's shipbuilders and sailors, and their craft, the flat-bottomed *gabarres, chalands* and *sapines.*
25km (15 miles) east of Orléans on the Loire. Musée de la Marine de Loire: Tel: 02 38 46 84 46. Open: daily except Tue; Nov–Mar 2–6pm, Apr–Oct 10am–6pm. Admission charge.

Château de Cheverny

The ancestors of Charles-Antoine, Marquis de Vibraye, who now lives at Cheverny, built the first castle some seven centuries ago. Nothing now remains of the earlier fortress: what visitors tour is a majestic mansion of white stone, familiar to fans of the *Tintin* cartoons as Moulinsart, the (imaginary) home of Captain Haddock. There is a permanent Tintin exhibition in the former smithy. Cheverny is also known for its hunting tradition. The kennels house a pack of 100 brown-and-white hounds, a cross between English foxhounds and Poitevins.

From a distance, the façade looks plain; closer inspection reveals busts of 12 Roman emperors in niches between the first-floor windows, and a 13th, Julius Caesar, in the gable above the central doorway. The guided tour begins in the dining-room, dominated by a table seating 30; castors of bone allow each chair to glide into place. Above, the silver-plated bronze chandelier looks modern but is 200 years old and weighs 100kg (220lbs). The walls are covered in leather, with 34 paintings detailing the tale of Don Quixote.

Climbing upstairs, you will pass the antlers of a massive prehistoric moose, hung at its estimated height, 3m (10ft) above the floor. The 17th-century armoury holds battle armour, a pirate's chest and the miniature breastplate and helmet of the five-year-old Comte de Chambord. All grand châteaux had to have a Chambre du Roi, in case the king came to stay. Although King Henri IV did sleep in this bed, it was not in this room but in the earlier château on this site. Downstairs in the grand salon are 17th- and 18th-century paintings, including work by Titian and Mignard, while the gallery is furnished with Regency chairs and portraits by Clouet, and the petit salon hung with 16th, 17th and 18th-century works. The château is surrounded by a very scenic 100ha (247-acre) park full of mature trees. In World War II, the Orangery in the garden was used to shelter French art treasures, including the *Mona Lisa*.

65km (40 miles) southwest of Orléans, 13km (8 miles) south of Blois. Tel: 02 54 79 96 29. www.chateau-cheverny.com. Open: daily. Admission charge.

Busts of Roman emperors line the façade of the Château de Cheverny

Cléry-Saint-André

Medieval pilgrims thronged here after a statue of the Virgin Mary was found in a bush in 1280. The original church was razed by the English in 1438 but Louis XI (1423–83) revived the shrine, pledging his weight in silver to the Virgin. His skull, and that of his wife, are locked away in a glass case; under a nearby stone is the heart of their son, Charles VIII, who finished the rebuilding.

15km (9 miles) southwest of Orléans on the D951. For guided tours, contact the presbytery at 1 rue du Cloître, next to the basilica (tel: 02 38 45 70 05).

Château de la Ferté-Saint-Aubin

This offers more than many other Loire Valley châteaux. The big draw is the

The church of Germigny-des-Prés is reputedly the oldest in France

TARTE TATIN

Lamotte-Beuvron, a pleasant little town in the Sologne, 35km (21 miles) south of Orléans, is where the Tatin sisters 'invented' their famous caramelised apple tart in the 1850s – by mistake, like so many famous dishes.

On discovering that the pastry to line the dish had been forgotten, Caroline spread it on top of the apples, butter and sugar. After baking, she inverted the pie and discovered . . . Tarte Tatin. Now Gilles Caillé, at the Hôtel Tatin, opposite the station, produces a dozen a day, using locally grown reinette, clochard or golden apples. Tradition insists that there should be no cream, no jam and no flambéing.

cookery demonstration in the vaulted, stone-floored, 17th-century kitchen. A log fire blazes, game and vegetables are heaped on the massive work table, and the cook, in bonnet and apron, conjures up *terrines* and *tartes tatins* (*see box*) using the gleaming copper pots. Outside, the petting zoo and the real horses in the historic stables occupy the children while the adults tour the 18 rooms of the 16th-century château.

18km (11 miles) south of Orléans on the N20. Tel: 02 38 76 52 72. Open: mid-Mar–Sept, daily 10am–7pm, mid-Feb–mid-Mar 2–6pm. Cooking demonstrations daily Apr–Sept, but phone to check. Admission charge.

Germigny-des-Prés

Germigny-des-Prés has one of the oldest surviving churches in France. It dates back to AD 806 and is beautifully decorated with 130,000 gold, silver and blue cubes of glittering glass to form a Byzantine picture of the Ark of the Covenant, guarded by the Hand of God and four angels. In the squat lantern tower above the altar thin panes of translucent alabaster, rather than glass, fill the windows.

28km (17 miles) southeast of Orléans on the Loire. Tel: 02 38 58 27 03. Open daily. Donation appreciated.

Mennetou-sur-Cher

Mennetou is a town of steep and twisting streets set within 800-year-old walls, still standing over 12m high. The Porte d'en Bas is often called the Porte Jeanne d'Arc, for she stopped here on 3 March 1429, on her way to Chinon to see the Dauphin (*see pp88–9*). The Grande-Rue is actually a narrow lane, lined with ancient houses, including the tourist office, which occupies a 16th-century layer-cake of sandy stone and half-timbering, topped with red tiles, next to another massive gate.

85km (50 miles) south of Orléans on the N76.

Meung-sur-Loire

'Remember poor Villon,' the poet and rascal, François Villon (*see p96*) implored his friends from the castle dungeon. He was reprieved in 1461, by Louis XI, but hundreds of less-fortunate inmates died here. Take a look at the *salle de question* (a euphemism for torture chamber) and the *oubliettes*, where 'forgotten' prisoners starved to death. Most of the rest of the château was remodelled in the 18th century. The village, where the Mauve River splits into rivulets and channels before joining the Loire, is also known for the 13th-century poet, Jean de Meung, who added 18,000 new lines to the *Roman de la Rose* (written by Guillame de Lorris around 1240). His satirical style criticised the conventions of courtly love and morals of self-indulgent priests. It's no wonder it was hugely popular.

22km (13 miles) southwest of Orléans on the N152. Tel: 02 38 44 36 47.

The Porte d'Amont, Meung-sur-Loire

Country life: an elegant sitting-room in the remote Château du Moulin

www.chateaudemeung.com.
Open: Mar–Oct daily; Nov–Feb
Sat–Sun. Admission charge.

Château du Moulin

Off the beaten tourist track, this château has a wide moat, drawbridge and towers with loopholes, crenellations and machicolations. It is, however, more country mansion than fortress. At the battle of Fornovo di Taro, in 1495, Philippe du Moulin saved the life of Charles VIII; the grateful monarch awarded his captain the privilege of fortifying his home. The two surviving buildings sit on a large, square terrace. Inside, 14th-century tapestries hang in the main bedroom and the main salon has a painted ceiling, while pewter flagons and platters sit on a heavily carved sideboard. There is even an original spit, which would once have been powered by a dog.
65km (40 miles) southwest of Orléans
off the D765, near Lassay-sur-Croisne.
Tel: 02 54 83 83 51. Open: Apr–Oct
Thur–Tue. Admission charge.

Quincy and Reuilly

These two neighbouring, and somewhat undistinguished, villages produce good but little-known wines. The best from Quincy are the dry white Sauvignons, made in the Sancerre style. Reuilly produces reds, whites and rosés and has a wine festival in the first weekend of April.
Quincy is on the west bank of the Cher, 104km (64 miles) south of Orléans. Reuilly is on the D198, 110km (68 miles) south of Orléans.

Romorantin-Lanthenay

Built on and around an island in the Sauldre River, the 'capital of the Sologne' offers pleasant walks by old watermills and crooked streets lined by 15th- and 16th-century timber-framed houses. Head for the rue du Milieu where, at the Maison du Carroir d'Orré, a carved St George raises his sword to slay the dragon. Nearby, the Hôtel St-Pol is a handsome mixture of glazed bricks and stone. It was here, on 6 January 1521, that François I was up to some high jinks when he was hit on the head by a burning log. The 26-year-old king grew a beard to hide the scar, and set a new fashion. Opposite, La Chancellerie boasts a finely carved bagpiper. The **motor racing museum** shows locally built blue Matra racing cars.

The **Museum of Sologne** customs and traditions is housed in a converted watermill.
65km (40 miles) south of Orléans on the D922. L'Espace Automobiles Matra:

17 rue Capucins. Tel: 02 54 94 55 58.
www.museematra.com.
Open: Mon–Fri 9am–noon, 2–6pm; Sat
& Sun from 10am. Admission charge.
Musee de Sologne: Tel: 02 54 95 33 66.
www.museedesologne.com.
Open: Wed–Mon. Admission charge.

Saint-Benoît-sur-Loire

Dominating the village is the massive
abbey church of Saint-Benoît, the final
resting place of St Benedict (480–547),
the father of western monasticism. The
Italian saint died at Montecassino, near
Naples, but when that monastery was
sacked, his remains were transferred to
this site in AD 672. The present church
was built between 1067 and 1218.
Twelve massive pillars support the
bell-tower-cum-porch, each heavily
carved with scenes from the Book of
Revelations. The design reflects John's
vision in Revelations 21, with three
doors or arches to the east, west, north
and south. The interior of the church,
73m (240ft) long and 20m (65ft) high,
is a model of Romanesque simplicity,
solid and impressive. The recumbent
statue of Philippe I of France
(1052–1108) lies by the altar, and
steps down to the darkened crypt
on the left lead to St Benedict's
relics, housed in a brass-bound
metal chest. The monks offer guided
tours, and it is well worth staying for
one of the six daily services in
Gregorian chant.
40km (25 miles) southeast of Orléans off
the D952. Tel: 02 38 35 72 43.
www.saint-benoit-sur-loire.fr

East Central Loire

The picturesque Romorantin-Lanthenay is situated on and around an island

The covered porch of the church at Souvigny-en-Sologne

Selles-sur-Cher

A small town with big ideas, Selles promotes itself as a holiday base. Less than an hour's drive from a dozen famous châteaux, it also invites anglers to try the four waterways that flow round and through the town. The dilapidated-looking moated château, now privately owned, is under repair.

The former abbey church, with its energetic sculptures, is the burial place of Selles' patron saint, Eusice, who arrived in the 6th century. Inside, take time to admire the stained-glass windows that relate the miracles of the saint. In the crypt is his tomb, which is regularly visited by pilgrims. In the main square, the simple **Cher Valley Museum** of local life focuses on basket-weaving, flint-cutting and the fine local goat's cheese. The flat round discs, salted and dusted in crushed charcoal,

are well-partnered by local wines, red or white.

100km (62 miles) southwest of Orléans off the N76. Musée du Val de Cher: Tel: 02 54 95 25 40. Open: Jun–Aug daily. Admission charge.

Souvigny-en-Sologne

This Sologne hamlet is famous for its characteristic half-timbered and red-brick houses and its church, which has a vast red-tiled roof and unusual 16th-century *caquetoir* (covered porch, so-called because female parishioners gathered here to gossip after attending the service).

37km (23 miles) southeast of Orléans, east of Lamotte-Beuvron.

Sully-sur-Loire

Sully is a microcosm of French history, boasting a roll-call of famous residents.

One was Maurice de Sully, a poor local priest who went to Paris, became bishop and commissioned the building of Nôtre-Dame cathedral. Three centuries later, Jeanne d'Arc arrived to take the Dauphin, Charles VII, to Reims to be crowned.

The town's heyday came after Maximilien de Béthune (1560–1641), Henri IV's chief minister, bought the estate and became the Duc de Sully in the early 17th century. Like a modern tycoon, he was up before sunrise, with a rota of secretaries recording his orders. Learned in law and accountancy, he had a secret printing press installed in one tower to print his memoirs, entitled *Wise and Royal Economies of State*.

His **château** is undergoing constant restoration, which actually adds to the interest of a visit. The first floor was converted into a theatre when an 18th-century descendant of the duke welcomed the banished 22-year-old playwright, François-Marie Arouet, to his home. Arouet later adopted the pen-name Voltaire, and he wrote several plays here in the early 1700s. At night the moated castle is lit dramatically by floodlights.
41km (25 miles) southeast of Orléans on the D948.
Château: Tel: 02 38 36 36 86.
www.loiret.com. Open: Feb–Dec daily.
Admission charge.

Château de Talcy

Two women inspired two different poets in this delightful fortified Gothic-style manor, which began life as a *donjon*. The first was Cassandra, the 15-year-old daughter of Tuscan banker Bernardo Salviati, who bought the château in 1517. Ronsard (1524–85) dedicated over 180 of his frustrated love poems to this 'nymph'. Salviati's grand-daughter, Diana, had the same effect on Agrippa d'Aubigné (1552–1630) who dedicated his poem *Le Printemps* (*Springtime*) to her. Fine furniture fills the Renaissance rooms, which are furnished in 17th–18th-century style. Gothic tapestries decorate the guard room, salons and bedrooms; the cellar has an ingenious mechanical wine-press, still in working order; a well-preserved 16th-century dovecote stands in the second courtyard.
40km (25 miles) southwest of Orléans off the A10, D70. Château:
Tel: 02 54 81 03 01. Open: daily.
Closed: Tue (winter). Admission charge.

The château of Sully-sur-Loire

By bike: the Sologne

The once marshy, but now drained, Sologne has long been a mysterious part of France. Today, the region is famous for hunting. Its red-brick villages are quiet and unspoiled and, because it is flat, cycling is straightforward.

Allow 2 days or, taking the shortcut indicated, one long day.

Start in Lamotte-Beuvron, by the railway station.

1 Hôtel Tatin

Tarte Tatin, the famous apple tart, originated here (*see p100*). A wedge of this should fortify any cyclist.
Head north, past the town hall. Take the D101 for Vouzon, through the Lamotte-Beuvron forest.

2 Vouzon

The houses here are of warm-coloured brick with red-tiled roofs.

Turn right before the church, still on the D101. In summer, the roadside is ablaze with purple heather.

3 Souvigny-en-Sologne

This village of 400 inhabitants has a photogenic church, built between the 12th and 17th centuries. A sharp spire juts from the red-tiled roof; the well-preserved *caquetoir* (*see p104*) dates from the 16th century. Among the surrounding half-timbered houses are some good restaurants.
Take the D126 for Chaon.

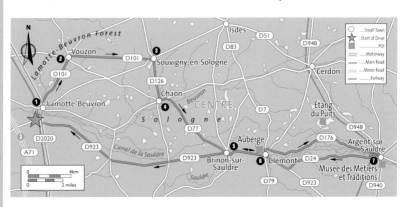

The Sauldre River near Brinon

4 Chaon

The road leads through pleasant countryside, past a château with half-timbered stables, ponds and picnickers. Chaon is another pretty red-brick village.

Continue on the D126, then turn on to the D77 for Brinon.

5 Brinon-sur-Sauldre

Children are often to be seen swimming in the Sauldre River, which flows through the village and into the Cher. The church, set on a rise, has a distinctive spire, a deep-sweeping roof and another *caquetoir*.

From here, it is possible to take a short cut back to Lamotte-Beuvron via the D923. Otherwise, stay on the D923 to Clémont.

6 Clémont

A giant grain elevator signals the entrance to Clémont, which is just off the main road, set round a triangular village green. The 14th-century church is unusual in this area in that it is built of stone rather than brick. Admire the delicate sculptures and magnificent entrance on the west side.

To the right of the Auberge, take the D176 towards Cerdon, but turn sharp right along the river for Argent-sur-Sauldre, beneath shady plane trees.

7 Argent-sur-Sauldre

On the left, the 100-year-old **Étang du Puits** is both bird sanctuary and leisure park, with windsurfers on the lake. Enter Argent by crossing both the canal and the river to find two rival *auberges*, both covered with flowers. In the château, the old-fashioned but interesting **Musée des Métiers et Traditions** (Trades and Traditions Museum) commemorates the everyday life of the *ventres jaunes* (yellow bellies), which is what the Sologne people are nicknamed. Discover the uses of strange-looking implements such as the *tourniquet de bébé* – not a medical tool but a baby walker.

Return to Clémont on the D24, south of the river, then via Brinon back to Lamotte-Beuvron on the D923.

The charming, quiet attraction of the grounds of the Château de Villesavin

Château de Troussay

A century ago, the historian Louis de la Saussaye set out to save treasures from dilapidated mansions. His collection, including Renaissance stained glass and a stone carving of a porcupine from Blois, now enlivens his manor house near Cheverny. A small museum of Sologne life is housed in the outbuildings.

70km (43 miles) southwest of Orléans off the D765, 3.5km (2 miles) west of Cheverny. Tel: 02 54 44 29 07. Open: Easter–Sept daily 10am–noon & 2–6pm. Admission charge.

Château du Valençay

Charles-Maurice de Talleyrand-Périgord, better known simply as Talleyrand, purchased Valençay in 1803, when he was Napoleon's Foreign Minister, and he used the château to entertain dignitaries from all over Europe. After the fall of Napoleon, negotiations under the Congress of Vienna (1814–15) were held here to redraw the map of Europe. A bedroom with Talleyrand's own furniture is adjacent to the room occupied by Ferdinand VII of Spain while confined here by Napoleon. The fine gardens have black swans, deer, peacocks and cranes.

Nearby is the **old car museum** which displays 60 classic cars, the earliest from 1898, all in working order.

115km (71 miles) southwest of Orléans on the D956. Tel: 02 54 00 10 66. www.chateau-valencay.fr. Open: Apr–Oct daily. Admission charge.

Son et Lumière shows in Jul, Aug & Sept (tel: 02 54 00 04 42 for details).

Musee de l'Automobile: Route de Blois. Tel: 02 54 00 07 74. Open: daily except mornings Dec–Feb. Admission charge.

Vendôme

Now a mere 40 minutes from Paris by TGV, the so-called 'gateway to the Loire' honours the famous people who lived here with a bust of the 16th-century poet, Ronsard, in rue St-Jacques, and a statue on the place St-Martin of the Comte de Rochambeau, who helped the American colonists defeat the British at the Battle of Yorktown in 1781. The 19th-century author Honoré de Balzac spent miserable schooldays here, but still used the town as a setting for such novels as *Louis Lambert*.

Remnants of the medieval era include the castle on the hill and La Trinité Church, founded by the Count and Countess of Anjou after seeing a vision of three flaming spears (or shooting stars) in 1035. The 80m-bell tower, with its 11-ton bell, dates from this early church, but the west front is an outstanding example of Flamboyant Gothic architecture, with stonework that really does look flame-like. The most arresting of the stained-glass windows is the 12th-century *Virgin and Child* at the eastern end; most fun are the carved angels and devils on the misericords, in the choir.

Part of the Abbey houses the **Musée de Vendôme** with its remarkable collection of porcelain, furniture from the 16th and 18th centuries and Marie-Antoinette's harp.

76km (47 miles) southwest of Orléans on the N10. Musée de Vendôme: Tel: 02 54 77 26 13. Open: Apr–Oct Wed–Mon, Nov–Mar Wed–Sat & Mon. Admission charge.

Château de Villesavin

Villesavin was built between 1526 and 1537 by Jean le Breton, the financial advisor to François I and superintendent of the building works at nearby Chambord. Now, a bumpy driveway leads to his small château, which encloses a courtyard with a white Carrara-marble basin, carved by the same Italians who built the rest of the charming Renaissance building. The original dovecote is in excellent condition, complete with ladder and 1,500 nesting boxes.

60km (37 miles) southwest of Orléans, near Bracieux. Tel: 02 54 46 42 88. www.chateauvillesavin.com. Open: Feb–Oct daily, weekends in Nov & Dec. Closed: Jan. Admission charge.

St George's Gate: home of Vendôme's Council Chamber for 400 years

Tour: the Cher

This route explores a short, quiet stretch of the south bank of the Cher. The river is 367km (228 miles) long, but this drive is only some 87km (54 miles), from Vierzon to Montrichard (see map on p85).

Allow at least half a day.

1 Vierzon

This dull, industrial town has hidden corners of interest. Known today for its porcelain, it has long been a watery intersection where the Yèvre meets the Cher. In the old town, narrow streets lined with medieval houses lead to the 12th-century church of Nôtre-Dame.

Go south on the D918, then the D918e, following signs for Saint-Hilaire-de-Court and then Saint-Georges-sur-la-Prée. Continue on the D50 and D51 to Saint-Julien. On the way, note the dramatic Anjou-style spire of the Saint-Loup church (inside are 13th-century murals).

2 Saint-Julien-sur-Cher

The peace and quiet of Saint-Julien contrasts with its neighbour Villefranche, across the bridge, where lorries constantly rumble through on the main road.

Continue on the D51, then take the D35 to Chabris.

3 Chabris

Chabris is a jolly little village, with a riverside campsite under the trees where children dive into the Cher. Rent a bicycle and pedal by the river, have a glass of Sauvignon wine and local goat's cheese or go dancing at the *guinguette*, the dance hall-cum-café. Saint-Phalien, a 5th-century hermit, is buried in the church, which boasts unusual carvings.

Continue on the D35, then take the D51 to Selles.

4 Selles-sur-Cher

Famous for its goat's cheeses, the town has several half-timbered houses as well as the remains of the 6th-century hermit, Saint-Eusice, buried in the crypt of the 12th-century church (*see p104*). Step inside to admire the stained-glass windows that depict the miracles of the town's saint. The former Abbaye Royale houses a Museum of the Cher with displays on the local boatmen and the making of goat's

On guard for 1,000 years: Foulques III Nerra's keep at Montrichard

cheese. Sadly, the château here has reverted to being a private residence and is predictably closed to the public. *Take the D17 to Saint-Aignan, passing through Meusnes which, for 300 years, was the centre of the gunflints industry.*

5 Saint-Aignan-sur-Cher

Saint-Aignan's church is a mix of Norman and Gothic architecture with intricately carved pillars and, in the vast crypt, 12th-century frescoes depicting miracle cures worked by medieval saints. The particularly high 11th-century crypt is well-known for the collection of wall paintings. These well-preserved, vibrant murals date from the 12th, 15th and 16th centuries. The town's 16th-century château is closed to the public, but its courtyard offers a vista over the town's medieval rooftops. Getting there involves a climb of 114 steps up a curving, stone staircase. *Continue on the D17 to Pouillé.*

6 Pouillé

This wine-producing town is surrounded by Touraine vineyards, devoted to growing Sauvignon Blanc and Gamay grapes. Pouillé's Gamay Festival is held on the last weekend in July. *Continue on the D17 and cross the bridge to Montrichard.*

7 Montrichard

Above the town (*see p70*) stands the restored keep of Foulques III Nerra, where Richard the Lionheart was besieged by Philippe-August in 1188. The graffiti on the walls were left by the Knights Templar in 1308. The Church of Sainte-Croix hosted the ill-fated marriage of Jeanne, the deformed daughter of Louis XI, and the Duc d'Orléans, later Louis XII. *Return to Tours on the D40, on the northern bank of the Cher, or the faster N76, on the southern bank.*

The Eastern Loire

Bourges, famous for its majestic cathedral, one of the greatest Gothic creations in France, is the largest city in the Eastern Loire. Bourges and the surrounding region of Berry are surprisingly overlooked when it comes to visitors. 'Many French aren't sure where we are,' admits one local, 'they think we're further south.' But this area is the centre of France and is not short of history.

The city is also associated with Jacques Coeur (1400–56), skilful financial adviser to Charles VII. His is one of the finest medieval mansions in France but there are plenty of others, albeit less grand, on the cobbled streets of the old quarter.

The countryside around Bourges has few 'attractions' in the tourist sense. The flat Sologne is popular with hunters, and it has several churches with *caquetoirs* (porches 'for gossiping'), surrounded by red-brick cottages. Sancerre and Pouilly are renowned around the world for their flinty, dry white wines.

The region also has its surprises. One is the iron canal aqueduct that spans the Loire at Briare; another is the 16th-century bridge, with 10 arches, at nearby La Charité. Turn up in Aubigny-sur-Nère in mid-July and you will hear the skirl of the pipes and see the lilt of the kilt as Scottish visitors confirm the Auld Alliance; the Verrerie, a nearby château, was built by one John Stuart, who battled with the French against the English.

Another château, at La Bussière, is devoted to all aspects of angling, while the early owners of the château at La Chapelle d'Angillon discovered a tax loophole that today's accountants would relish. The work of the craftsmen potters at La Borne contrasts with the stylised designs on the faience of Gien. Deep in the country, Nançay offers art galleries and a gentleman's

---

THE DUC DE BERRY

The beautifully illuminated calendar, known as *Les Très Riches Heures du Duc de Berry*, depicts several places in the Loire Valley that are recognisable even today. First comes January, with the Duc de Berry himself seated at a well-laden dining-table, surrounded by a retinue dressed in the latest medieval fashion. September depicts the *vendange* (grape harvest) below the château at Saumur. Created by the Limbourg brothers and paid for by their patron, Jean, Duc de Berry (1340–1416), the original is now preserved at the Musée Condé in Chantilly, north of Paris.

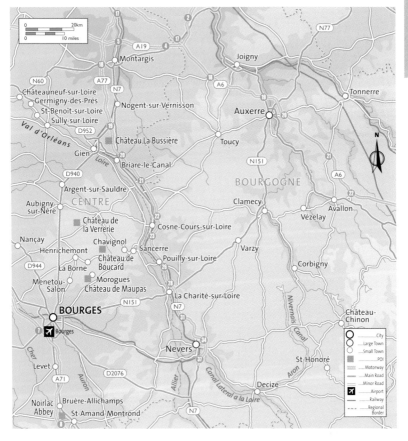

tailor catering to chic Parisians on weekend getaways. At the eastern extreme of the area is Nevers, a town worth a visit in its own right, but often overrun with pilgrims visiting the convent where St Bernadette (of Lourdes fame) lies embalmed.

Bourges

Only in 1992, when Bourges cathedral was named a World Heritage Site by UNESCO, did this well-preserved medieval city finally get its deserved share of the limelight. Until then, even the French thought of Bourges as being 'dans la France profonde', deep in provincial France. Part of this lack of recognition is due to the city fathers of 150 years ago who rejected the offer of a railway line. Even today, there are only two direct trains a day to Paris.

Bourges is much more than its cathedral, however: the city was

(Cont. on p116)

Royal ministers

The kings Charles VIII, Louis XII and François I played key roles in the Loire Valley. Evidence of the strong influence the monarchy had, both on the economy of the region and on the architecture of its towns, is clearly visible even today. However, there were also several leading ministers to the monarchy who were also very influential and had a hand in shaping the history of the Loire Valley.

The chapel of Trois Sainte Trinité in Richelieu

Jacques Coeur (c.1400–1456)

'*A vaillans coeurs, riens impossible*' (To brave hearts, nothing is impossible); so ran the punning motto of one of the most powerful men in France. As counsellor to the king, he reformed the tax system and put France back on her financial feet after the drain of the Hundred Years War. Coeur married well and he rose to become one of the richest men in Europe. His ships brought back silks and spices from the Middle East and he was soon in favour with Charles VII, and had a powerful ally in the king's mistress, Agnès Sorel,

Coeur was less popular with royal courtiers when he took land and property from them as payment for outstanding debts. In 1450, however, he was arrested, found guilty of supplying arms to the Muslims (infidels) and exiled. His entire fortune was confiscated. Coeur escaped from prison in Poitiers and fled to Rome. He died fighting in Rhodes against the Turks. Four years later, Louis XI threw out the court decision and returned Coeur's property to his family.

Cardinal Richelieu stands at the entrance of the town of Richelieu

Cardinal Richelieu (1585–1642)

Born Armand Jean du Plessis in Paris, Cardinal Richelieu became prime minister of France in 1624. Widely admired for his intelligence and energy, he is credited with being the person who released France from the limitations of a medieval mentality. During his service as prime minister under King Louis XIII, France emerged as the leading power in Europe. The Sorbonne in Paris, which supported promising writers and thinkers, was one of his projects. Another was the town of Richelieu (*see p74*). In 1631 he received permission from the king to build himself a palace and also a new walled town. Richelieu commissioned the famous architect Lemercier. The palace, which was ravaged during the Revolution, occupied 2,000 labourers for over a decade. The walled town remains intact.

Maximilien de Béthune (1560–1641)

Minister of Finance for Henri IV, Maximilien de Béthune, Duc de Rosny contributed to the rehabilitation of France after the long years of the Wars of Religion. With the motto 'hard work is the lifeblood of France' he encouraged agricultural and public works and set about building a network of roads and canals. He was given the title of Duc de Sully and acquired the château and town in 1602.

BURGHERS OF BOURGES

The people of Angers are called Angevins; those in Tours are Tourangeaux; in Orléans, they are Orléanais. In Bourges you might expect them to be Bourgeois but, in fact, they are Berruyers.

founded by the Romans and was later the capital of Aquitaine. In the 14th and 15th centuries, Bourges benefited from royal patronage. Nothing remains of the magnificent palace built by Jean, Duc de Berry (1340–1416), the brother of Charles V. The Duke was a lover of luxury and culture, and his tubby effigy marks his tomb in the cathedral crypt. His great-nephew, the weak, uncrowned Charles VII, was forced to flee here from Paris. He was mockingly nicknamed the 'Little King of Bourges', whereas Henry VI of England was called the 'King of Paris' because of his legitimate claim to the French throne and his control over most of France.

Bourges, however, remained a centre of resistance to the English in the final years of the Hundred Years War, even before the arrival of Jeanne d'Arc. The king's financier, the merchant banker, Jacques Coeur, planned to live here and he built a mansion as fine, if not finer, than any royal palace (though he never actually spent a night under its roof). The city's commercial power matched that of Lyon and Rouen and its university was founded in 1463. John Calvin, the Protestant reformer, studied here in the 16th century, when new theological ideas from Germany were

taking hold in France. As elsewhere, the Wars of Religion took their toll, with a fire in 1487 that destroyed much of the city.

Today, Bourges is still a capital, but only of the *département* of Cher. With a population of 100,000, it is a compact city whose April festival, Printemps de Bourges (Bourges Spring), focuses on French song. The economy depends on modern industries such as aeronautics, electronics, tyres and armaments; the last is nothing new, since Jacques Coeur traded arms to the Middle East as early as the 15th century.

Cathédrale de Saint-Étienne

On statistics alone, the cathedral is enormously impressive: 124m (406ft) long, 41m (134ft) wide and 37.5m (123ft) high with 1,000sq m (10,000sq ft) of stained glass. Saint-Étienne stands shoulder-to-shoulder with Notre-Dame de Paris, Chartres and Reims as a jewel of Gothic architecture, thanks to the consistency of style, intricate stone carving and the richly coloured 13th- and 15th-century windows.

The harmony was achieved by the speed of construction: most of the building went up in a mere 60 years, beginning in 1195, but was finally finished in 1324. Today, only the disparate height of the towers spoils the symmetry. Stand in the boulevard de Strasbourg in the morning to appreciate the *chevet* (the eastern end of the church) with its five radiating chapels and its two tiers of flying buttresses. Climb the 396 well-worn steps that lead to the top of the 65m (213ft)-high North (or Butter) Tower. From here, the nave really does look like an upturned ship.

Before going into the main entrance, stop and look at the west front. The Butter Tower, to the left, is so named because it was funded by 'indulgences' paid by affluent townsfolk for the privilege of eating butter during Lent. The 58m (190ft) Tour Sourde (Deaf Tower), on the right, got its name from being soundless – it never did have its bells installed. Both had spires which have collapsed; the Butter Tower has been rebuilt, while the Deaf Tower is supported by a buttress built in the 14th century.

The west façade is dense with sculptures. From left to right are the portals dedicated to Saint-Guillaume (a 13th-century archbishop of Bourges), the Virgin Mary, the Last Judgement, Saint-Étienne and Saint-Ursin, the first bishop of Bourges. The message of the Last Judgement is as clear now as it was to illiterate folk 800 years ago. Figures emerge from their tombs and clamber up to see what is happening on the next level. The Archangel Michael, smiling broadly, weighs the souls. To the left, off go the good souls to the bosom of Abraham; to the right, a delighted demon takes his victim to join the other unfortunates on their way to meet the devil. Monks are judged and found wanting; a toad pulls out tongues.

The view from the cathedral's North Tower

Graphic sculptures cover the west façade of Saint-Étienne

Inside, there are five naves to match the five portals. The late 14th-century west window features in *Les Très Riches Heures* (*see p112*). A copper strip set diagonally across the floor shows where the Paris meridian slices through the building, and a two-faced astrological clock dates from 1424. In the choir, the triumphant sense of light and space is due to the delicate pillars being slightly staggered. Between 10 and 11am on a sunny morning, the sun pours through the 12th-century stained-glass windows, which feel almost close enough to touch. These, too, have tales to tell. Some were sponsored by local guilds, such as the butchers or furriers, and illustrate appropriate events in the Bible. The story of the Prodigal Son, sixth from the left, has figures dancing the *pavane*, cheek to cheek. High above

the altar, two faded cardinal's hats hang from the roof. Local lore has it that the cardinals will languish in purgatory until the hats eventually rot and fall to the ground, when they will finally enter paradise. In the crypt, stonemasons work on the never-ending task of maintaining the building. Among the archbishops buried here is the recumbent marble effigy of Jean, Duc de Berry, guarded by a bear.
Open: daily. Guided tours (lasting 2 hours) mid-Jul–end Aug.

Hôtel Cujas (Musée du Berry)

This fine mansion was built in 1515 for a Florentine cloth merchant. Today it houses the Musée du Berry, best-known for its local Roman finds and Egyptian mummies. Here, too, are the *Pleurants*, mourning statues, which once

surrounded the tomb of Jean, Duc de Berry, carved in the 14th century but remarkably modern in their simplicity.
4-6 rue des Arènes. Tel: 02 48 70 41 92. Open: daily except Tue & Sun morning. Admission charge.

Hôtel des Echevins

Dramatically lit at night, this plain 15th-century L-shaped building, with its elaborate eight-sided stair turret, was built as a meeting place for the city aldermen. It is now a showcase for the work of the local contemporary artist, Maurice Estève and his vibrant, striking canvases.
13 rue Edouard de Branly. Tel: 02 48 24 75 38. Open: daily except Tue & Sun morning. Admission charge.

Hôtel Lallemant

This Renaissance mansion is built on the remains of the Roman city wall.

The broad entrance steps enabled horsemen to ride directly into the main courtyard, which is decorated with pottery plaques of classical heroes. In the family chapel, the ceiling is carved with alchemical symbols. This well-restored building is now a museum devoted to the decorative arts, ranging from tapestries and faience to fine examples of carved, inlaid and lacquered furniture.
6 rue Bourbonnoux. Tel: 02 48 57 81 17. Open: daily except Mon & Sun morning. Admission charge.

Palais Jacques-Coeur

Despite being unfurnished, this is one of the most interesting mansions in the whole of the Loire Valley. Jacques Coeur spent an estimated 100,000 golden *écus* building his grand home. Arraigned in 1451, he never had a chance to enjoy it. From

Saint-Etienne: one of Europe's most stunning cathedrals

The imposing Palais Jacques-Coeur

the strongroom (complete with secret locks) to the kitchens, the architecture is ingenious and includes a number of innovations remarkable for their time. There is even a steam bath and stone toilet. The fine Galerie des Marchands, with its beamed, boat's keel roof, stands next door to the private chapel, where angels fly across the ceiling. In the dining-hall, the stone fireplace is as monumental as any in the region. Coeur's business ethic – *Dire, Faire, Taire* (Speak, Do and Be Silent) – is carved on the east façade of the palace. *rue Jacques-Coeur. Tel: 02 48 24 79 42. Open: daily. Admission charge.*

Argent-sur-Sauldre

In this quiet Sologne village, the 15th-century château houses the **Musée des Métiers et Traditions de France** which looks at the ingenuity of the locals, nicknamed *ventres-jaunes* (yellow bellies) because of endemic jaundice. Their useful inventions include spiked collars to protect dogs from wolves, clogs elevated on spikes to keep feet dry in marshy conditions, and a charcoal-fuelled ancestor of the washing-machine.

57km (35 miles) north of Bourges, on the D940. Museé des Métiers et Traditions de France:
Tel: 02 48 73 33 10.
Open: Easter–mid-May Thur & Fri 2–6.30pm, Sat & Sun 10am–noon, 2–6.30pm; mid-May–Oct Mon & Wed 2–6.30pm, Thur–Sun 10am–noon, 2–6.30pm. Admission charge.

Aubigny-sur-Nère

On the weekend nearest Bastille Day, 14 July, the street parade through this *Cité des Stuarts* (Stuart City) includes twirling medieval banners and the *tricolore* of France, plus skirling bagpipes, swishing kilts and flags of St Andrew, celebrating the Auld Alliance victory against the English in 1419. During the 18th century, Jacobite refugees also settled here. All is explained in the town's small museum, dedicated to the alliance. Specially designed tartan, combining the colours of the town's shield with those of the Stuarts of Atholl, is for sale.

Centre d'Exposition de l'Auld Alliance: Tel: 02 48 81 50 07. Open: Jul–mid-Sept daily, mid-Sept–Jun weekends only. Admission charge.

(*Cont. on p124*)

Detail: Palais Jacques-Coeur

Walk: old Bourges

The heart of Bourges has many fine medieval half-timbered houses. These are being slowly refurbished as local people realise the attractions of living here.

Allow 45 minutes.

Start in front of the main entrance to the cathedral.

1 Cathédrale de Saint-Étienne

Spend a few minutes admiring the west front of this 13th-century Gothic building and imagine how vivid the Last Judgement carvings must have seemed to the populace of the Middle Ages.

Walk along the north side of the cathedral, turning into the rue des Trois Maillets, past the 13th-century Grange des Dîmes, where tithes were stored. Turn left into the pedestrianised rue Bourbonnoux.

2 Rue Bourbonnoux

Half-timbered houses dating from the 15th and 16th centuries line the cobbled street. Many, like no 77, are antique shops; others are restaurants and some are private homes. The palette and easel hanging outside no 33 signify that this is an art gallery; opposite, at no 34, the sign of the violin shows that a repairer of musical instruments works here. Look up above no 16: a *trompe l'oeil* shows a little girl peering down. The most photographed house is Aux Trois Flûtes, on the corner of rue Joyeuse. On the left, opposite, is the 15th-century Hôtel Lallemant, now the **Museum of Decorative Arts**.

Map of old Bourges with locations marked:

- Hôtel Pelvoysin
- 3 RUE MIRABEAU
- Musée Estève
- École des Beaux-Arts
- PLACE PLANCHAT
- PLACE GORDAINE
- BLVD G CLEMENCEAU
- Musée Berry
- PLACE CUJAS
- 5 Museum of Decorative Arts
- RUE COURSARLON
- Palais Jacques-Coeur
- PLACE JACQUES-COEUR
- RUE BOURBONNOUX
- Municipal Theatre
- RUE MOYENNE
- 2
- Musée de l'École
- R DES TROIS MAILLETS
- Maison de Jacques-Coeur
- 6
- RUE D'AURON
- 1 Cathédrale de St-Étienne
- PLACE DE LA PRÉFECTURE
- RUE VICTOR HUGO
- Musée des Meilleurs
- 7 Préfecture
- Cité Administrative
- Hôtel de Ville
- PLACE DU 8 MAI 1845
- RAMPE MARCEAU
- PLACE A MALRAUX
- Maison de la Culture
- AVENUE EUGÈNE BRISSON
- 0 — 100 metres
- 0 — 100 yards
- N

Legend:
- POI
- Start of Walk
- Cathedral
- Information
- Police Station

In place Gordaine, with its outdoor cafés, look to the left, down another medieval street, rue Coursarlon. Exit from the square, turning left on to rue Mirabeau.

3 Rue Mirabeau

Look above the street level boutiques to appreciate the detail of the 15th- and 16th-century houses.
Turn left on to rue Pelvoysin.

4 Rue Pelvoysin

A bank now occupies the Hôtel Pelvoysin, named after the 16th-century architect and built at an angle to catch more light.
Come out on to place Planchat; turn left on to rue du Commerce and right on to rue Jacques-Coeur.

5 Place Jacques-Coeur

Place Jacques-Coeur is named after Charles VII's finance minister (*see p114*), whose statue stands in the square, looking across to his palatial 15th-century home, Palais Jacques-Coeur. Above the main entrance, small statues of Coeur and his wife lean over as if to greet visitors. Note his coat of arms, which is a play on his name: it contains a heart (*coeur*) and a pilgrim's shell (the symbol of Saint-Jacques, or St James, of Santiago de Compostella).
Across the square on the right is the Municipal Theatre. Continue straight on to rue des Armuriers.

6 Rue des Armuriers

Legend has it that Jacques Coeur was born in 1400 in the house on the

corner with rue d'Auron, now a *pâtisserie*. In fact, the house dates from the 16th century.
Enter place de la Préfecture.

7 Place de la Préfecture

The administrative headquarters of the *département* of Cher occupy the 18th-century building on the right. This was the site of the Ducal Palace of Jean de Berry, where the future King Louis XI was born in 1423. Continue past the imposing offices and fountain into avenue H Ducrot. On the right, the ancient half-timbered house squashed between its neighbours is not a museum but a private home, complete with television aerial.
Turn left on to rue Victor-Hugo, which will take you to the tourist office.

Local lore: the cake shop which is supposedly Jacques Coeur's birthplace

Learn about life in the Sologne in the château at Argent-sur-Sauldre

Château de la Verrerie

Little of John Stuart's 15th-century castle survives; the brick Renaissance gallery, with its nine arches, and the murals in the chapel were added by his descendant, Robert Stuart. When the family died out in 1670, Louis XIV gave the château to the Duchess of Portsmouth, mistress of Charles II of England – himself a Stuart. More impressive than in photographs, the romantic setting by the reflecting lake supposedly inspired scenes in *Le Grand Meaulnes*, by local author Alain-Fournier (*see p126*). The current owners, the Comte and Comtesse de Vogüé, offer upmarket dinner-bed-and-breakfast accommodation.

10km (6 miles) southeast of Aubigny on the D89. Château: Tel: 02 48 81 51 60. Open: Mar–Nov Sat & Sun, Jul–Aug daily. Admission charge.
Aubigny is 50km (31 miles) north of Bourges on the D940.

La Borne

Over 400 years ago, the local abundance of clay and wood made La Borne a centre for the making of everyday stoneware vessels. This tradition died out, only to be reborn in the 1940s when a new generation of artists settled here. Among the first were Monsieur and Madame André Rosay, who continued making pottery in the peasant style, known as *art populaire*. Vassil Ivanoff created clay figures and shapes. Now some 50 craftsmen from nine countries work in and around what is a creative, if not pretty, village. The Centre de Céramique, in the former girls' school, displays contemporary works. Individual studios are open to visitors.

37km (23 miles) northeast of Bourges on the D22. Tel: 02 48 26 96 21. Open: daily. Free admission.

Chateau de Boucard

The River Sauldre fills the moat of this fierce-looking 15th-century castle, whose Renaissance courtyard is more welcoming. The rooms have 17th-century furniture and a mechanical spit stands idle in the kitchen while, in the chapel wall, a window built 200 years ago allowed the Princesse de la Trémoille to 'attend' services without leaving her room. Recitals and concerts are given here as part of the July Festival de Boucard.

40km (25 miles) northeast of Bourges off the D923. Tel: 02 48 58 75 49. Open: Apr–Nov Fri–Wed. Admission charge.

Briare-le-Canal

The 19th-century engineer Gustave Eiffel is best-known for the Tour Eiffel in Paris, but his Pont-Canal at Briare is also a technological wonder. This aqueduct carries the Canal Latéral across the Loire to join the Canal de Briare. Stylish, Parisian-style obelisks serve as lamp holders, guarding each end of the bridge, whose 663m (2,175ft) length is the longest in Europe. Known as the Ruban d'Eau (Ribbon of Water), the aqueduct took seven years to build (1890–97) and finally fulfilled Henri IV's dream of linking the Mediterranean to the English Channel using a network of rivers and canals. Visitors can stroll the length of the canal or cruise along it in a *bateau-mouche*. Like many small towns in the area, there is a tradition of enamelling.

75km (46 miles) northeast of Bourges.

The canal at Briare

Château La Bussière

Another of the region's more intimate châteaux, this early 17th-century gem was once incredibly wealthy: the huge barn on one side of the courtyard was built to hold tithe payments from vast estates in the area. The château has subsequently acquired the nickname of the Château des Pêcheurs, the Fishermans' Castle, because the Chasseval family owners have collected a mountain of angling memorabilia, including paintings and porcelain, rods and flies and even a stuffed coelacanth. The château stands on a little island in a lake and the grounds, landscaped by Jean le Nôtre, have been restored, along with the 18th-century *jardin-potager* (vegetable garden).

85km (53 miles) northeast of Bourges on the N7. Tel: 02 38 35 93 35. Open: Jul & Aug daily, late Mar–Jun & Sept–early Nov Wed–Mon. Admission charge.

La Chapelle d'Angillon

This little known town was the birthplace of Henri Alain-Fournier (real name Henri-Alban Fournier, 1886–1914), son of a schoolmaster and author of the romantic and semi-autobiographical novel, *Le Grande Meaulnes* (1913), known in English as *The Lost Domain*. He was killed at Saint-Remy soon after the outbreak of World War I. Inside the exterior of the town's **Château de Béthune** is a small museum dedicated to the author. The chapel, with its Luca della Robbia *Madonna and Child* is still filled on a Sunday morning. The Chambre du Roi, where Henri IV and Louis XIV both slept, has a fine painting of St Stephen by Murillo. The Duc de Sully bought the estate 300 years ago because it included the Principality of Boisbelle, which was exempt from all taxes. The current Count wishes it still were!

32km (20 miles) north of Bourges. Tel: 02 48 73 41 10. Open: daily except Sun morning. Admission charge.

La Charité-sur-Loire

The eccentric name recalls the generous monks who helped pilgrims on their way to and from Santiago de Compostella, in northwest Spain. The abbey church of Nôtre-Dame, consecrated in 1107, was second in size only to that at Cluny and it is still impressive, despite damage from a fire in 1599. The place des Bénédictines, off the Grande Rue, offers a good view of the red-tiled *chevet* (east end of the church), and the slate-roofed Tour de Bertrange; unfortunately it is too far away to decipher the carvings.

The town has retained its medieval character, so it is worth wandering through the narrow streets to the ramparts overlooking the Loire, spanned by a 16th-century 10-arched bridge. Some houses are gabled, others recycled from the abbey complex. Jeanne d'Arc paid a visit in December 1429.

52km (32 miles) east of Bourges on the N151.

Chavignol

This attractive village, wedged between the Sancerre vineyards, is the production centre for one of France's best goat's cheeses, still made to a recipe recorded as early as 1573. The curds from raw goat's milk are moulded, then salted individually. After 12 days, they are known as *bleutés* because of the slightly bluish skin. Left for 20 days, they become *très secs* (very dry). Stored for longer in a crock-pot, they become *repassés* (well-aged). At this point, they are round brown balls, nicknamed *crottins* for their resemblance to horse dung. Gourmets argue the merits of each type – over a glass of Sancerre, of course.

50km (31 miles) northeast of Bourges, just west of Sancerre off the D955.

Gien

Badly damaged in World War II, much of the rebuilding of Gien, from its smart quays and 16th-century bridge to houses of brick and pale stone, has been carried out in a sensitive manner. The Centre Anne de Beaujeu, named after Charles VIII's business-like sister, who built the hilltop church, was reconstructed in brick after 1945. The church itself, dedicated to Joan of Arc, has faience panels on the outside recording her four visits in 1429. Next door, the colours of the red, black and white brickwork on the castle reflect the proximity of Burgundy, while the lifesize statue of a stag symbolises the **Hunting Museum** inside. This displays horns, crossbows,

A moment of reflection: La Charité-sur-Loire with its 16th-century bridge

Bricks and mortar: Gien has been heavily restored and rebuilt

stuffed bears and boars and some 70 paintings by Louis XIV's official hunt painter.

Gien is best-known for its high-quality faience, painted with traditional animal, bird and flower patterns – even the street signs are made of the tin-glazed earthenware, introduced in 1821 by an Englishman.

Musée de la Faiencerie de Gien: place de la Victoire. Tel: 02 38 05 21 06. Open: daily except mornings in Jan & Feb. Admission charge. Musée International de la Chasse: Château de Gien. Tel: 02 38 67 69 69. Open: Jul–Aug daily, Sept–Jun Wed–Mon. Admission charge.

78km (48 miles) northeast of Bourges off the D940.

Henrichemont

The Duc de Sully (*see p126*), planned to build a Protestant enclave here, named after the king he served (*Henrici mons* means Henry's Hill). Unlike Richelieu (*see p115*), it was never completed. Today, only the eight streets radiating from the main square of this dull town hint at the 17th-century design.

27km (16 miles) northeast of Bourges off the D940, D11.

Menetou-Salon

Menetou-Salon is near Sancerre, but has its own *appellation contrôleé* red, white and rosé wines. The château was built in 1450 by Jacques Coeur, Charles VII's finance minister (*see p114*). The restoration a century ago was inspired by his house in Bourges and paid for by Prince Auguste d'Arenberg, president of the Suez Canal Company. The wonderful collection of vintage cars includes an 1899 Panhard Levasseur.

20km (12 miles) northeast of Bourges on the D11. Tel: 02 48 64 80 16. Open: Jul, Aug & Sept daily. Admission charge.

Morogues

This commune in the Menetou-Salon wine-growing area boasts the 14th-century **Château de Maupas**, which deserves a visit. The Maupas family were administrators to the Duchess of Berry and her son, the Comte de

Chambord, pretender to the French throne. This explains the souvenirs relating to France's final flirtation with the restoration of the monarchy only a century ago. Surprisingly, there is no local faience in the 887-piece collection of plates lining the staircase.

25km (15 miles) northeast of Bourges on the D59. Tel: 02 48 64 41 71. Open: Easter–Sept daily. Admission charge.

Nançay

The sophisticated shops here come as a surprise, until you learn that chic Parisians spend weekends in this village. Local author Alain-Fournier (*see p126*) holidayed here at the turn of the century and the château may have been the setting for the party scene in his novel, *Le Grande Meaulnes*. Today it houses an arts and crafts gallery, open at weekends. Sablé de Nançay biscuits are the local delicacy, and one of the world's largest radio telescopes is hidden in the woods.

35km (21 miles) northwest of Bourges on the D944.

Nevers

Thousands of pilgrims flock to the Convent of St Gildard, northwest of the city. In 1866, Bernadette Soubirous, later St Bernadette, arrived here from Lourdes to join the Sisters of Nevers. She died here in 1879, aged 35; her body is on view in a glass casket. Bernadette was canonised in 1933 and a summer 'musical' based on her life was inaugurated in 1995.

Like Gien, Nevers is known for faience, made here since 1648. Although the town museum explains

The grandiose plans for Henrichemont were never completed

Ancient and modern: new stained glass in Nevers' medieval cathedral

the making of this tin-glazed stoneware, most visitors head for the Bout-du-Monde shop on rue de la Porte-du-Croux (visits to the workshop need to be made by reservation; *tel: 03 86 71 96 90*).

The city's architectural highlights include the church of Saint-Etienne, the Porte-du-Croux city gate, the cathedral of Saint-Cyr-et-Sainte-Julitte and the Ducal Palace.
69km (43 miles) southeast of Bourges.

Noirlac Abbey

Even though Noirlac lies just outside the boundaries of this guide, the 12th-century white stone abbey is worth a detour. The restored church, cloisters and chapter house, on the banks of the Cher, were built for the Cistercian order, founded in 1098 to get back to

the monastic basics of prayer, austerity and simplicity. Cistercian abbeys, often situated in isolated valleys, had no stained glass, paintings or sculpture. A special exhibition here explains the significance of gestures in medieval miniatures, while the summer concerts are particularly atmospheric.
Bruère-Allichamps, 40km (25 miles) south of Bourges off the A71 motorway. Abbey and concert details. Tel: 02 48 62 01 01. Open: daily. Closed: Jan. Admission charge.

Pouilly-sur-Loire

This unremarkable town produces a remarkable wine: Pouilly-Blanc-Fumé (not to be confused with Pouilly-Fuissé in Burgundy). Grapes have been grown here for 1,500 years. The town's current fame dates back to the 19th-century planting of the Sauvignon Blanc variety. The *fumé* (smokiness) supposedly refers to the *pierre-de-fusil* (gunflint) flavour that pundits love. Pale in colour, and very dry, Pouilly wines should be drunk young. White meats and fish are perfect partners.

57km (35 miles) northeast of Bourges.

Sancerre

Downstream from Pouilly, the hilltop town of Sancerre has more character, but experts disagree about the merits of the two wines (like that of Pouilly, Sancerre is also made from the Sauvignon Blanc grape). The ramparts and circular Tour des Fiefs recall the seven-month siege of the Wars of Religion (*see p57*). Today, white stone houses line the streets while the sloping Nouvelle Place is the place to buy arts and crafts, wine, local goat's cheeses and tasty biscuits such as *palettes sancerroises* (with nougat and orange peel).

Rue Macdonald honours another group of Scots; these fled with Bonnie Prince Charlie and settled here in the mid-18th century. Halfway down, a plaque commemorates a descendant, one Étienne-Jacques-Joseph-Alexandre, who became Marshal Macdonald, one of Napoleon's most trusted military leaders. From the Esplanade de la Porte César, there is a sweeping northeasterly view over the Loire.

47km (29 miles) northeast of Bourges.

Lush vineyard at Sancerre

The Upper Loire

'We've seen the châteaux, so we've done the Loire.' Anyone who thinks this has forgotten that there is still the Upper Loire, a region with its own beauty and history.

South of Nevers, on the N81, the ruins of Rozemont castle are a slowly decaying memory of the Hundred Years War. The Aron River and the Nivernais Canal join the Loire at Decize, where the Promenade des Halles is a splendid 900m- (2,952ft) long avenue of ancient plane trees. Further upstream, the Loire meanders to Digoin, with its 15-arch bridge and another confluence of canals. Roanne, dating back to Roman times, was the highest point upstream regularly navigable by boats. Today, this prosperous town is a place of culinary pilgrimage, thanks to Pierre and Michel Troisgros, whose restaurant (Troisgros, in place Gare) is one of France's finest.

The heart of the Loire Valley

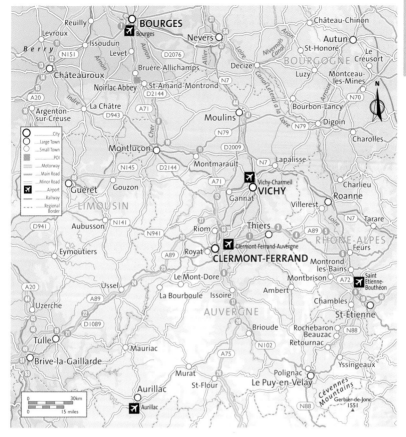

Villerest marks the start of the 30km- (18-mile) long, rapid-filled gorges of the Loire. At the Saut de Perron, the rocks have evocative names: the Stairway, the Wolf and the Black Rock. Feurs and Montrond-les-Bains come next in what is a flat, marshy stretch of the river. The delicate blue Fourme d'Ambert cheese, sold in the local markets, comes from the nearby hills.

At Chambles, the Loire is close to Saint-Étienne, where coal mined centuries ago was floated downstream on rafts made of *sapins* (pine logs). From here the river passes a chain of small towns: Rochebaron with its castle; medieval Beauzac and Retournac, standing high above the river.

La Voûte and Polignac boast castles and Le Puy-en-Velay has a dramatic cathedral, with the Black Virgin at the high altar. The final stretch, up to the source, is a twisting, steep climb towards Mt-Gerbier-de-Jonc, 1,000km (621 miles) from the Atlantic Ocean.

Getting away from it all

There are countless ways to enjoy and explore the Loire or the other major rivers that have sculpted the landscape in this part of France. Take to the water or the air for a different perspective and walk or cycle along the banks or tow paths for a more intimate view and greater understanding of the rivers' significance.

Aerial views

The châteaux of the Loire and the river itself look superb from the air. Hot air balloon flights are at dawn or dusk but weather-dependent.

France Montgolfières
Tel: 02 54 32 20 48. Phone for launch locations and deals.
www.franceballoons.com

Boat trips

With hundreds of kilometres of rivers and canals in the region, holidays afloat are popular. Boats are available for hire at the following centres:

Sarthe, Mayenne and Oudon rivers
From Château-Gontier:
Tel: 02 43 70 37 83.
From Sablé-sur-Sarthe and Malicorne:
Tel: 02 41 95 93 13.
From Grez-Neuville: *Tel: 02 41 95 68 95; www.anjou-navigation.com*

On the Loire River
From Montjean: (hire an old *gabare*, the traditional Loire sailing boat).
Tel: 02 41 72 81 81.

On the Erdre River
From Nantes: *Tel: 02 40 14 51 14.*

On the Sèvre River
From Nantes: *Tel: 02 40 14 51 14.*

Cycling

The Loire *à vélo* long distance cycling route offers around 800km (500 miles) of easy cycling through the Pays de la Loire and Loire Valley. Cycle paths are well signposted and straightforward to follow: there are leaflets at tourist offices or check online,
www.loire-a-velo.fr

Hiking

The French network of long-distance footpaths is well organised and well marked. The national paths are called **Grandes Randonnées**, or GR, and are numbered for identification. The **Fédération Française de la Randonnée Pédestre** (FFRP) has drawn up excellent maps and guides called *Topo-Guides*. Local tourist offices can advise on where to hike in their area. The best-known walk across the region is GR3, the **Sentier de la Loire** (the Loire Path). The main section, from Orléans to Saumur, is some 255km (158 miles) long and links Beaugency and Chambord, Chaumont and Amboise, Vouvray and Tours, Azay-le-Rideau and Chinon. *FFRP: 14 rue Riquet, 75019 Paris. Tel: 01 44 89 93 93; www.ffrp.asso.fr*

The coast

After exploring the gentle landscape and cultural attractions of the Loire Valley, many families look to head to the coast in search of sun and sea. From Nantes it is around 150km (95 miles) to La Rochelle, a picturesque and historically rich seaport on the Bay of Biscay. Europe's largest pleasure boat marina is here at Les Minimes. Other attractions include a large aquarium, a maritime museum and a small botanical garden. The old town is well preserved and packed with seafood restaurants. The city is connected to the Île de Ré by a 3km (2-mile) bridge. The 30km by 5km (18 by 3 mile) island is a popular tourist destination and has as many hours of sunshine as the southern coast of France. The gently sloping, sandy beaches are the main draw and the island is criss-crossed with bicycle tracks for exploring. Fresh fish and oysters are always on sale on the quay as well as in local restaurants, as is the island's famous ice cream.

Gardens and parks

Although the Forêt d'Orléans lies to the east, only smaller woodlands now remain of the old royal hunting reserves of Amboise, Chinon and Loches. What the Loire Valley does have, however, is gardens. The art of French gardening was born here in the 16th century, when Italian Renaissance culture influenced not just architecture and interior decoration but also the

The harbour at La Rochelle

Perfumed gardens at Chamerolles are a highlight

design of gardens. The 17th century brought the most famous landscape gardener of them all, André Le Nôtre, creator of the gardens at Versailles.

Today, the gardens of most of the grand châteaux are open to the public, and so are several private ones, though often for just a few weeks each summer. It is always worth telephoning ahead to see if there are any guided tours, which can make the visit even more enjoyable for amateur botanists.

Angers

The **Jardin des Plantes** (on the northeastern edge of the city, on place Mendès-France) is best known for its English-style gardens and first-class displays of rhododendrons, and is home to some rare species of tree; the **Aboretum Gaston Allard** (on rue du Château d'Orgement) also houses exotic trees from around the world.
Tel: 02 41 23 50 00. Open: daily. Free admission.

Bourges

The **Jardin des Prés Fichaux** in the north of the city was opened in 1930 and still has a real Art Deco look about it, thanks to the numerous statues dotted along the paths and among the clipped hedges. The formal gardens behind the cathedral, the Jardin de l'Archevêché offer good views of the 15th-century chapel spires.
Blvd de la République. Tel: 02 48 23 02 60. Open: daily. Free admission.

La Bussière

The 17th-century Château gardens, designed by Le Nôtre, have been re-created and the 18th-century kitchen garden flourishes.
85km (53 miles) northeast of Bourges. Tel: 02 38 35 93 35. Open: see p126. Admission charge.

Chamerolles

Perfume is the theme of the **Château de Chamerolles** and of its geometrical Renaissance garden, where the flowers are planted for their scent.
At Chilleurs-aux-Bois, 30km (18 miles) northeast of Orléans. Tel: 02 38 39 84 66. Open: Wed–Mon. Closed: Jan. Admission charge.

Chanteloup

Chanteloup in the forest of Amboise has a 44m- (144ft) high Chinese style pagoda, but nothing else remains of the splendid Versailles-style château destroyed in 1823. The gardens have been restored according to the original plans.

2km (1 mile) south of Amboise.
Tel: 02 47 57 20 97. www.pagode-chanteloup.com. Open: daily,
Easter–Sept. Admission charge.

Châteauneuf-sur-Loire

The 86ha (212-acre) park surrounding
the remains of the château is another
Le Nôtre masterpiece, although it was
redesigned in 1821. The best known
feature is the 800m- (2,625ft) long
rhododendron walk, which is in its
pomp in late May and early June.
Tel: 02 38 58 41 18. Open: daily.
Free admission.

Chaumont-sur-Loire

An annual festival – an international
challenge to gardeners from all over the
world to create a themed garden – is
held here. It has included a Zen garden
and a 'poor man's garden' planted with
just three packets of seeds.
Tel: 02 54 51 26 26.
www.chaumont-jardins.com.
Open: see p60. Admission charge.

Chemillé

The **Jardin des Plantes Médicinales**,
in the grounds of the town hall, has
over 300 varieties of medicinal herbs
and plants.
30km (18 miles) southwest of Angers.
Tel: 02 41 30 35 17. Free admission.

Cheverny

Giant sequoias (redwood trees) are
among the rarities in the 100ha
(247-acre) 17th-century gardens.
65km (40 miles) southwest of Orléans.
Tel: 02 54 79 96 29. Open: daily.
Admission charge.

Doué-la-Fontaine

In the town nicknamed City of
the Roses, for its huge industry,
the **Jardin des Roses** has over 250
varieties. The town's flower show,
Journées de la Rose, takes place
annually in July.
40km (25 miles) southeast of Angers.
Tel: 02 41 59 20 49. Open: daily.
Free admission.

New England in old France: American entry in Chaumont's garden festival

Château d'Ussé is straight out of a fairy tale

La Ferté-St-Aubin

The garden, with its ancient cypress trees and delightful mixture of islands, water and moats hosts a spring festival. *18km (11 miles) south of Orléans. Tel: 02 38 76 52 72. Open: see p100. Admission charge.*

Maulévrier

The 28ha (69-acre) **Parc Oriental** claims to be the biggest Japanese garden in Europe, complete with temples, bridges, a pagoda and a wooden summer house. A path marked with Japanese lanterns circles a lake and explores the grounds. *12km (7 miles) southeast of Cholet. Tel: 02 41 55 50 14. www.parc-oriental. com. Open: Mar–Jun, Sept & Oct Tue–Sun; Jul & Aug daily; Nov–Feb Tue–Sun afternoons only. Admission charge.*

Montoire-sur-le-Loir

The **Parc Botanique de la Fosse** at Fontaine-les-Côteaux is the pride of the family who have introduced thousands of exotic trees and plants since 1751. *50km (31 miles) northeast of Tours. Tel: 02 54 85 38 63. Open: all year weekend afternoons; Jul & Aug Wed–Fri. Admission charge.*

Nogent-sur-Vernisson

Trees are the stars in the 100-year-old **Arboretum National des Barres**, one of France's finest collections. *60km (37 miles) east of Orléans. Tel: 02 38 97 62 21. Open: mid-Mar–mid-Nov Tue–Sun, winter Mon & Fri afternoons. Admission charge.*

Orléans

The city's **Jardin des Plantes** is 150 years old and has fine greenhouses and an orangery. The rose-garden and flowerbeds are beautifully maintained. The peaceful **Parc Louis Pasteur**, opened in 1927, has neat flower beds, trees and shrubs (*tel: 02 38 49 30 00; open: daily; free admission*).

Out at Orléans-la-Source, the **Parc Floral** combines a wildlife park with

30ha (70 acres) of roses and dahlias, bulbs and irises. The Loiret rises in the grounds (*tel: 02 38 49 30 00; www.parc-floral-la-source.com; open: daily; free admission*).

Talcy
Well-tended château grounds replanted with rare species of fruit trees.
40km (25 miles) southwest of Orléans.
Tel: 02 54 81 03 01. Open: daily.
Closed: Tue Oct–Mar. Admission charge.

Tours
The **Jardin Botanique** is famous for its magnolia walk and its new hothouses devoted to orchids and passion flowers. The **Jardin des Prébendes d'Oé** was designed in 1857 by the Bülher brothers as a city garden with a pond, bridge, cypress and cedar trees.

Perfect symmetry and organisation in the garden at Villandry

Tel: 02 47 21 68 18. Both gardens are open daily. Free admission.

Ussé
The Château d'Ussé boasts formal gardens designed by Le Nôtre.
40km (25 miles) southwest of Tours.
Tel: 02 47 95 54 05. Open: see p76.
Admission charge.

Valençay
With topiary and real animals, including deer, llamas and kangaroos, the gardens surrounding the Château de Valençay appeal to those interested in garden design.
115km (71 miles) southwest of Orléans.
Tel: 02 54 00 10 66. Open: see p108.
Admission charge.

Vernou-sur-Brenne
The beautifully kept Renaissance gardens surrounding the Château de Jallanges stretch for 7ha (17 acres).
10km (6 miles) northeast of Tours.
Tel: 02 47 52 06 66. Open: Mar–Oct daily. Admission charge.

Villandry
Arguably the most famous château garden in France: designed by Dr Joachim de Carvallo, it has ornamental, water and lovers' gardens. To appreciate the geometric patterns, stand on the terrace behind the château or on top of the keep.
15km (9 miles) west of Tours.
Tel: 02 47 50 02 09. Open: daily.
Admission charge.

Shopping

In addition to the gift shops in each of the châteaux, there are plenty of places to pick up a present or lasting memento of your trip, whether you're looking for confectionery or chocolate, wine or other local produce, trinkets or tapestries. Specialist shops are everywhere and local markets provide yet more opportunities to buy the things for which the Loire is famous.

SHOPPING FOR FOOD

Boucherie: the butcher's shop, where everything but pork is sold (by tradition, the *charcuterie* handles pork). Closed on Mondays.

Boucherie chevaline: the horse's head outside shows that this is a horse butcher. Open Mon–Sat.

Boulangerie: perhaps the most important shop of all, since the French buy their bread fresh at least twice a day, for lunch and dinner. The long, familiar loaf is a *baguette* but *pain intégral* (wholemeal bread) is common nowadays, as is *pain de campagne*, a heavy white country bread, or *pain de seigle*, a slightly sour rye bread, good with cheese. The sign '*depôt de pain*' denotes shops that sell bread, but do not bake it.

Charcuterie: the *charcutier* once dealt only with the pig and its by-products, such as sausages, terrines and patés. Nowadays the *charcuterie* looks more and more like a delicatessen.

Confiserie: sells sweets made on the premises. Beautifully displayed and wrapped chocolates are always a feature.

Epicerie: literally a spice shop, but nowadays the grocer's, carrying almost everything.

Fromagerie: the best cheese shops are run by *affineurs*, who mature the cheeses they buy from the farmer and sell them at peak condition.

Pâtisserie: cake shops full of home-made tarts and ice cream, pastries and cakes. Many sell home-made chocolates, too.

Poissonnerie: the best fishmongers often smoke fish and make fish patés and fish soup.

Traiteur: sells ready-made dishes to take home.

Triperie: common in the north of the region, where tripe is a popular delicacy (it often tastes better when cooked by a specialist).

In the Loire Valley, the high quality of the food shops matches that of the vintners. It is, therefore, the perfect place to indulge the taste buds and discover local specialities.

Amboise

Since 1913, the **Pâtisserie Bigot** has sold sweet things and offered afternoon tea in an atmospheric old house opposite the entrance to the château.
place du Château. Tel: 02 47 57 04 46.

Angers

At **La Petite Marquise,** Michel Berrué makes his award-winning *Quernons d'Ardoise*, blue squares of chocolate-coated nougatine that deliberately resemble slates from the local quarry.
22 rue des Lices.
Tel: 02 41 87 43 01.
www.chocolat-lapetitemarquise.com

La Chartre-sur-le-Loir

This is the sort of 'local shopping' that makes other nationalities feel jealous of the French. Fun to look as well as to buy and try, all round the main square.

Window shopping in Saumur

La Flèche

Another small town where the local specialities are prepared with pride and skill.

Nantes

The **Pâtisserie Débotté** here is a wonderful pâtisserie which is also a salon de thé.
rue Crebillon. Tel: 02 40 69 03 33.

Orléans

The *macarons* (macaroons) at **Les Musardises** are legendary. Find this pâtisserie near the station.
38 rue de la République.
Tel: 02 38 53 30 98.

The **Chocolaterie Royale** is well over 200 years old. Among the specialities are the *Pralines Jeanne d'Arc.*
51 rue Royale. Tel: 02 38 53 93 43.

Tours

Unusual presentation stops window-shoppers in their tracks outside **La Chocolatière**, where chocolates come in decorative baskets or pottery dishes.
4 rue Scellerie. Tel: 02 47 05 66 75.

Au Vieux Four is more than a simple bread shop , with over 70 different types of bread, all made using organic flour and baked in the traditional wood-fired oven.
7 place des Petites-Boucheries.
Tel: 02 47 66 62 33.

Since 1807, **Poirault** has been an institution for cakes and tea. Ask to watch the sweets being made.
31 rue Nationale. Tel: 02 47 66 99 99.

The region is rich with locally made arts and crafts

SPECIALITY SHOPPING

The Loire Valley once catered to the tastes of kings and their courts. Those days are long gone but the area can still satisfy even the most dedicated of shoppers. Cities such as Angers, Tours, Nantes, Orléans and Bourges have a fine assortment of specialist shops, as do the towns of Saumur and Blois. Designer dresses, luxury foodstuffs and antiques shops are often to be found in pedestrianised zones; many stay open until 6 or 7pm. While food shops can be tempting in villages, other shops tend to be less exciting. The exception is Nançay, in the Sologne, where *tout Paris* (the Paris set) goes for weekends and shops for Scottish cashmere, jewellery and art.

Angers

The **Maison d'Adam** is a tourist sight in its own right. Inside, an exhibition centre and shop display the work of local craftsmen and artists.
1 place Ste-Croix. Tel: 02 41 88 06 27.

La Borne

Potters' workshops are open for visits throughout the summer in and around this hamlet near Henrichemont.
See pp124–5. Tel: 02 48 26 73 76.

La Coudray-Macouard

Robert Hamon makes *girouettes* (weather vanes). Order one shaped like your own house, or go for the traditional French cockerel.
Atelier de la Girouetterie, rue du Puits-Venier. Tel: 02 41 67 98 30.

Mehun-sur-Yèvre

The **Centre Régional des Métiers d'Art** is a showcase for over 200 painters, potters, jewellers and weavers.
les Grands Moulins. Tel: 02 48 57 36 84.

Orléans

Meubles Mailfert, the award-winning manufacturer of reproduction 17th- and 18th-century furniture, is located here in a historic house.
26 rue Notre-Dame de Recouvrance. Tel: 02 38 62 70 61.

Poncé-sur-le-Loir

An old mill is now the **Centre d'Art et d'Artisanat**, a crafts centre, where everything is made and sold on the premises, from pottery to hats and from glass to candles.
On the main road. Tel: 02 43 44 45 31.

Tours

The pedestrianised rue Colbert is renowned for antique shops. One of the most frequented is **Au Vieux Tours**, which is jam-packed with furniture and objects from the region. But don't expect to pick up a bargain.

Au Vieux Tours: 91 rue Colbert.
Tel: 02 47 66 73 94.

Villaine-les-Rochers

Basket-weaving has been a speciality since 1849 and the **Société Coopérative Agricole de Vannerie** is the place for buying handmade souvenirs.

1 rue de la Cheneillère.
Tel: 02 47 45 43 03.
www.vannerie.com

WINE SHOPPING

Choice is the only problem facing wine lovers in the Loire Valley, which boasts some 60 wine appellations and *Vins Délimités de Qualité Supérieure* (VDQS) areas. These have to satisfy high-quality standards laid down by the national controlling authority. With a wide selection, in all price bands, there is real scope for comparing and contrasting.

Market day in Amboise

MARKETS AND FAIRS

This 'garden of France' has abundant markets filled with fresh fruit and vegetables, local wines and cheeses.

Amboise	Wednesday, Friday and Saturday
Angers	Tuesday to Sunday
Azay-le-Rideau	Wednesday
Beaugency	Saturday
Blois	Wednesday, Saturday and Sunday
Bourges	Thursday, Saturday and Sunday
La Chartre-sur-le-Loir	Thursday
Château-Gontier	Thursday and Saturday morning
Chinon	Thursday
La Flèche	Wednesday and Sunday
Fontevraud	Wednesday and Saturday morning
Gien	Wednesday and Saturday morning
Langeais	Sunday
Loches	Wednesday and Saturday
Le Lude	Thursday
Montlouis-sur-Loire	Thursday
Montoire-sur-le-Loir	Wednesday
Montrichard	Monday and Friday
Nantes	Tuesday to Sunday
Orléans	Tuesday to Sunday
Richelieu	Monday and Friday
Romorantin-Lanthenay	Wednesday, Friday and Saturday
Sablé-sur-Sarthe	Monday and Wednesday
Sancerre	Saturday (all year), Tuesday (in March to November)
Saumur	Tuesday to Thursday and Saturday
Selles-sur-Cher	Thursday
Sully-sur-Loire	Monday
Tours	Tuesday to Sunday
Valençay	Tuesday
Vendôme	Friday and Sunday

Muscadet

Best drunk young, so avoid any 'bargains' that are over three years old. Look for the phrase 'sur lie', which means that fermentation took place on the lees leading to a fuller fruitiness and rounder flavour. The best houses include Louis Métaireau, Chéreau-Carré and Donatien Bahuaud.

Maison des Vins de Nantes, Bellevue

44690 La Haye-Fouassière. Tel: 02 40 36 90 10; fax: 02 40 36 95 87.

Anjou and Saumur

Some 25 appellations produce in excess of 11 million cases a year. For an overview, visit the special wine centres in Angers, opposite the castle, and in Saumur, near the river.

Maison des Vins d'Anjou et de Saumur

5 bis, place Kennedy, 49100 Angers. Tel: 02 41 88 81 13; fax: 02 41 86 71 84.

Maison du Vin, Saumur

quai Lucien Gautier, 49400 Saumur. Tel: 02 41 38 45 83.

Layon Valley

The Bonnezeaux and Quarts de Chaume are the most prized appellations of the sweet, white Côteaux du Layon wines. At their peak, they match the Sauternes of Bordeaux for quality, while undercutting them in price. Get acquainted with Layon wines at St-Lambert-du-Lattay, 20km (12 miles) south of Angers, where local growers take turns to display their wines.

Maison du Vin

Place Vignerons, 49750 St-Lambert-du-Lattay. Tel: 02 41 74 01 29. Open: daily in summer.

Saint-Hilaire-Saint-Florent

The main producers of the region's sparkling wines have their headquarters

Dégustation in a wine cellar

here, west of Saumur. 'A high-quality alternative to Champagne' says American wine guru Robert Parker of the wines produced at Bouvet-Ladubay, founded in 1851. Equally famous are Ackerman-Laurence and Gratien & Meyer.

Bouvet-Ladubay

1 rue de l'Abbaye, St-Hilaire-St-Florent, 49400 Saumur.
Tel: 02 41 83 83 83.
Open: daily. They also run a wine-school (www.bouvet-ladubay.fr).

Touraine

The red wines of Chinon at best can be excellent and long-lived. Producers such as Charles Joguet and Couly-Dutheil are outstanding, turning their Cabernet Franc grapes into complex, spicy, berry-scented wines at competitive prices. Also underestimated outside France are the still and sparkling white wines of Vouvray, east of Tours. At Gaston Huet's estate, traditional, semi-organic methods are used to produce wines extolled by the novelist Sir Walter Scott in 1827.

Domaine Huet

11–13 rue de la Croix-Brisée, 37210 Vouvray. Tel: 02 47 52 78 87.

Marc Brédif

Quai de la Loire, 37210 Rochecorbon.
Tel: 02 47 52 50 07;
fax: 02 47 52 53 41.

Cave des Producteurs

Brings together 50 wine-growers. The wines are bottled and matured in cellars in 1km of galleries dug into the rock. Free tastings.
38 La Vallée Coquette, 37210 Vouvray.
Tel: 02 47 52 75 03; fax: 02 47 52 66 41.

Sancerre and Pouilly-Fumé

Under pressure from New World winemakers, the producers of Sancerres have developed a new, fruitier style of wine, well represented by Henri Pellé and Jean-Max Roger. Traditional well-structured Sancerres are produced by winegrowers such as Vacheron, Paul Cotat and Lucien Crochet.

When it comes to Pouilly-Fumé, on the east bank of the Loire, JC Chatelain, Serge Dagueneau and Baron de Ladoucette, of Château du Nozet, are the star names.

Vacheron et Fils

1 rue du Puits Poulton, 18300 Sancerre.
Tel: 02 48 54 09 93; fax: 02 48 54 01 74.

Other wines

In the small town of La Chartre-sur-le-Loir, Joël Gigou makes rare Jasnières in both white and red versions.

Joël Gigou

4 rue des Caves, 72340 La Chartre-sur-le-Loir. Tel: 02 43 44 48 72.

In the Eastern Loire, Menetou-Salon, Quincy and Reuilly are little-known wines, but fine, light and quaffable.

Entertainment

Traditionally, entertainment in the Loire centres on cultured events at theatres or the opera or involves music festivals and recitals. However, the main towns, particularly those with large student populations, have nightlife in the form of clubs and bars. In summer, Son et Lumière (sound and light) spectacles are held at châteaux throughout the region.

BARS AND CLUBS

Bigger towns such as Nantes, Orléans and Tours boast the widest range of bars and clubs. Nightlife in other Loire towns centres on local café-bars or out-of-town discos.

Angers

L'Abbaye

Popular cocktail bar, with a decent range of beers too, is popular with students and the younger crowd.

41 Ayrault. Tel: 02 41 88 47 92. Open: Mon–Sat 3pm–2am, Sun 5pm–1am.

La Casa de Cuba

Cuban bar specialising in Salsa and Latin beats.

23 boulevard du Marécal Foch. Tel: 02 41 20 03 28. Open: Mon 6pm–2am, Tue–Sat 11.30am–2am, Sun 4pm–2am.

Amboise

Café des Arts

Basic but atmospheric bar between the château and Clos Lucé that sometimes hosts music nights.

32 rue Victor Hugo. Tel: 02 47 57 25 04. Open: Tue–Sun.

Le Shaker

More than 100 cocktails on offer along with a superb view of the château.

3 quai Francois Tissard, L'Ile d'Or. Tel: 02 47 23 24 26. Open: 6pm–3 or 4am. Closed: Jan and low season Mon.

Nantes

Place du Commerce and Place Royale have plenty of bars on offer. Elsewhere try **Café Graslin** (*1 rue Racine. Open: daily 4pm–2am*), which has a choice of 200 beers or **Café Cult** (*2 rue des Carmes. Open: Mon–Sat*), which is popular during the day. **Le Floride** (*4 rue st Domingue. Open: Wed–Sun 11pm–5am*) attracts a rock crowd to its open terrace. **Le Marlowe** (*1 place St-Vincent. Open: Mon–Thur 10.30pm–4am, Fri & Sat till 5am*) hosts a mix of music in a converted church. On l'Ile de Nantes, at the western tip, is **Hangar à Bananes**, a converted warehouse that features a number of bars and a nightclub that gets busy on Friday and Saturday evenings.

Orléans

There are a wealth of bars and watering holes in the heart of the pedestrianised part of the city around rue de Bourgogne. **L'Atelier** and **Le Bô Bar** are both good bets for a cocktail or aperitif, while **Le Paxton** is a decent approximation of a British pub. Alternatively, place du Martroi has a number of bars with outdoor terraces overlooking the busy square. **Le Coq Hardie** (_12 place du Chatelet. Open: daily till midnight_) is a particularly Gallic bar popular with locals.

Saumur

Le Saint-Cloud. Inviting terrace at this corner bar with a good wine list.
16 place Bilange. Tel: 02 41 51 25 81.

Tours

Place Plumereau is surrounded by bars that buzz in the evenings. **Café du Vieux Mûrier** (_see p166_) is the most reliably good. Close by at _36 place Grand Marché_, **Bar Le Tourangeau** is popular with locals. **Les Frères Berthom** at _5 rue Commerce_ is a bustling bar favoured by a younger crowd, who pack its terrace around happy hour. Rather smarter is **La Canteen** (_10 rue de la Grosse Tour. Open: 12–2.30pm and 7.30–11pm_), which has a wide selection of wines by the glass. **Le Café Chaud** (_33 rue Briçonnet. Open: 9pm–4am, closed Sun_)

and **Le Pacio** (_1 place de la Resistance. Open: daily 11pm–5am_) both have popular dance floors.

CINEMA
Angers
Les 400 Coups
Independent cinema showing films in the original language.
12 rue Claveau. Tel: 02 41 88 70 95.
www.les400coups.org

Tours
Studio
International films with French sub-titles.
2 rue des Ursulines. Tel: 02 47 20 27 00.
www.studiocine.com

Tours sur Loire
Terrace on the banks of the river, next to Pont Wilson; often shows open-air cinema but also puts on music events.
place Anayole Wilson. Open May–Sept.

Orléans
Les Carmes
Showing art house and international films in the original language.
7 rue des Carmes. Tel: 02 38 62 94 79.
www.cinemadescarmes.com

LIVE MUSIC
Angers
James Joyce
Irish pub that hosts regular live acts.
40 boulevard Carnot. Open: Mon–Fri 11.30am–1.45am, Sat 3pm–1.45am, Sun 4pm–1.45am.

Gargantuan celebrations at Chinon's Rabelaisian medieval market

Blois
Ben's Blues Bar
Live blues and gypsy-style jazz in this compact, atmospheric venue.
41 rue St Lubin. Open Thur–Tue 6.30pm–2am.

Velvet Jazz Lounge
Smooth jazz in a series of sumptuous thirteenth century vaults.
15 bis rue Haute. www.velvet-jazz-lounge.com. Open 5pm–2am, till 8pm Sun, closed Mon.

Nantes
0 Lodge
Regularly features performances by local bands.
place de la République.

Tours
Les Trois Orfèvres
Grungy rock dive with live bands and DJs.
6 rue des Orfèvres. Open: Wed–Sat 11pm–5am.

OPERA
Tours
Grand Théâtre
Hosts a wide programme of opera, orchestral performances and classical music recitals.
34 rue de la Scellerie. Tel: 02 47 60 20 20. www.operadetours.com

SON ET LUMIÈRE
The sound and light show was 'invented' by P Robert-Houdin in 1952 at Chambord. The idea was to bring the Loire châteaux to life, using recorded voices and lights playing on different parts of the building – a sort of radio drama with spotlights. Since then, it has developed into an art form, sometimes involving hundreds of local people, horses, boats and fireworks. They are an essential part of the Loire Valley experience.

Darkness is essential, so most shows start quite late (usually at 10pm). Shows are often limited to weekends and holidays. Check for dates, times, ticket availability and possibility of simultaneous translation in English on headphones. The local tourist office will give helpful tips.

Amboise

Visitors come to *La Cour du Roy François* (the Court of King François I) on Wednesday and Saturday nights to see 450 actors in Renaissance dress. *Tel: 02 47 57 14 47. www.renaissance-amboise.com*

Azay-le-Rideau

The spectacle entitled 'Les Imaginaires d'Azay le Rideau' relives Renaissance life in nine scenes around the grounds. *Tel: 02 47 45 42 04. Jul–Aug.*

Beaugency

The town puts on a historical spectacle for a week in summer. *Tel: 02 38 44 54 42.*

Blois

Ainsi Blois vous est conté (This is the Tale of Blois) at the château features images of important moments in the history of the château. *Tel: 02 54 90 33 32.*

Bourges

Follow the blue lanterns and take an illuminated journey through the medieval city of Bourges. Stop to listen to the text while admiring the architecture of the 'old town'. *Tel: 02 48 23 02 60.*

Chenonceau

A stunning walk through the gardens and grounds accompanied by extraordinary illuminations orchestrated by Pierre Bideau and backed by the music of Corelli. *Tel: 02 47 23 90 07.*

Loches

A spectacular night-time stroll around the illuminated monuments and medieval streets of the town, followed by a spectacle of fire and dance. *Tel: 02 47 59 01 32. Early Jul–late Aug.*

Le Puy-du-Fou

The history of the Vendée region from medieval times to the present day. This is the première Son et Lumière show with more than 1,000 actors, 250 horses, pyrotechnics and special effects. *Tel: 02 51 64 11 11. www.puydufou.com*

Saumur

Les Tuffolies (Tufa Follies) is an evening show using the château as a backdrop. *Tel: 02 41 51 03 06.*

Vouvray wines are stored in caves

Valençay

The château grounds are lit by 3,000 candles as a troupe of period actors perform atmospheric scenes.
Tel: 02 54 00 04 42.

THEATRE

Angers

Théâtre Le Quai

Opposite the château. Hosts theatre and live music events, with open-air performances in the summer.
17 rue de la Tannerie. Tel: 02 44 01 22 22. www.lequai-angers.eu

UNDERGROUND ATTRACTIONS

Many of the caves of the region, once excavated for their stone, have been recycled as wine cellars and mushroom farms. The most interesting are now restaurants and museums.

Le Coudray-Macouard

The Magnanerie du Coudray is a silkworm farm (the caterpillars grow between May and October) featuring an explanation of silk as a textile.
Impasse de Bel-Air. Tel: 02 41 67 91 24. Admission charge.

Dénezé-sous-Doué

More than 400 sculpted figures and faces are carved in the living rock, supposedly by 16th-century stonemasons evading persecution.
Tel: 02 41 59 15 40. Open: Easter–mid-Nov daily. Wed, musical evening. Admission charge.

La Fosse-Forges

A complete hamlet has been restored to allow visitors to imagine what daily life would have been like underground.
Tel: 02 41 59 00 32. Open: Mar–Oct daily. Admission charge.

Grézillé

The Clos des Roches is a carefully restored home, complete with bread oven, now used to make *fouaces* (hot bread) for the restaurant.
At Bourgneuf. Tel: 02 41 45 59 36. Reservation essential.

Le Monde Souterrain du Château de Brézé

A château beneath a château. Explore the galleries dug out of the stone. A subterranean world with bakery, kitchen and even drawbridge.
Tel: 02 41 51 60 15. Open: Mar–Nov daily. Admission charge.

Louresse-Rochemenier

The troglodyte village has some 20 rooms, furnished as they would have been at the turn of the last century. There is even a subterranean chapel.
Tel: 02 41 59 18 15. Open: Feb–mid-Nov daily. Admission charge.

The **Caves de la Genevraie** is an underground restaurant specialising in *fouaces* (hot bread, baked in a wood-fired oven).
Tel: 02 41 59 34 22. Open: Fri, Sat & Sun in general; longer in high season. Reservation essential.

Montsoreau

The Champignonnière at Saut-aux-Loups gives visitors the story of mushrooms, from cultivation to cooking pot. Afterwards, eat *galipettes* (big caps) stuffed and baked in a stone oven.

Tel: 02 41 51 70 30. Open: Feb–mid-Nov weekends & public holidays, Jul & Aug daily.

Parnay

The Château de Marconnay is one of the few troglodyte castles in the Loire region. Taste and buy wines in the cellars.
Tel: 02 41 67 24 14.
Open: Apr–Sept daily except Mon.

Rochecorbon

Les Hautes Roches is both a restaurant and a hotel, with rooms in the rock.
Tel: 02 47 52 88 88. Booking essential.
Expensive.

Saint-Georges-des-Sept-Voies

The Orbière is an underground sculpture by Jacques Warminski that has to be seen to be believed. Visitors tour the inside of this truly unique work of art, chiselled out of 90-million-year-old rock.

Tel: 02 41 57 95 92. Open: daily, except Oct–Apr mornings.
Admission charge.

Saint-Hilaire-Saint-Florent

A tour of the mushroom museum is delightfully cool on a hot day.
Route de Gennes. Tel: 02 41 50 31 55.
Open: mid-Feb–mid-Nov daily.

Troglo'Tap

Apples are dried and preserved as they were centuries ago. Watch – then eat.
Tel: 02 41 51 48 30.
Open: Mar–Oct weekends;
Jun–Sept daily except Mon.
Admission charge.

Vouvray

La Cave Martin serves regional dishes in a cave in the cliffs.
In hamlet of La Vallée Coquette.
Tel: 02 47 52 62 18. Booking essential.
Mid-price.

Dark secrets: troglodytic mushrooms

Children

'Not another château!' When you hear that cry from the back seat, you know it's time to take a break from castles. Luckily, the past 20 years have seen a real growth in the range of 'things to do' in the Loire Valley. Choose from zoos, underground caves, aquariums and slate mines, as well as a whole host of more traditional museums. Most have reduced rates for children.

Amboise

La Maison Enchantée is a house containing 250 automated figures arranged in 25 scenes from history and literature.
7 rue du Général Foy. Tel: 02 47 23 24 50. Open: daily. Closed: Mon in winter. Admission charge.

The **Musée de la Poste** includes stage coaches and carriages used by postal services around the world, as well as pictures, letters and stamps.
6 rue Joyeuse. Tel: 02 47 57 00 11. Open: Tue–Sun. Closed: Jan. Admission charge.

Angers

The **Musée de Pignerolle**, in the château, is based around the theme of communications – 'from tom-toms to satellites' – and includes a look at the history of electricity and television. Underrated and entertaining.
8km (5 miles) east of Angers. Tel: 02 41 93 38 38; www.museecomunication.org.

Open: Mar–Oct daily & Nov–Feb weekends. Closed: Jan. Admission charge.

Azay-le-Rideau

The **Musée Dufresne** is packed with 2,000 old military vehicles, tanks, cars, tractors, motorcycles and fire engines, some driven by steam, others by petrol engines, and a restored paddle-wheel. Picnic areas.
At Marnay, 5km west of Azay. Tel: 02 47 45 36 18. www.musee-dufresne.com. Open: daily. Closed: Dec & Jan. Admission charge.

Blancafort

The region of Berry claims to be the 'sorcery capital of France' and the **Musée de la Sorcellerie** tells the story of alchemists, elves, magicians and witches in scenes portraying the history and legends of the region.
12km (7 miles) east of Aubigny-sur-Nère. Tel: 02 48 73 86 11. Open: Easter–Oct daily. Admission charge.

Blois

Astrespace is an interactive museum of science and astrology.
18 rue Dorgeles. Tel: 02 54 42 02 95. Open: daily. Admission charge.

Plunge into the universe of illusion in the **Maison de la Magie** museum of magic devoted to inventor and wizard Robert Houdin.
Place du Chateau. Tel: 02 54 55 26 26. www.maisondelamagie.fr. Open: daily, Oct–Mar Mon only. Admission charge.

Château de Valençay

This is one of the châteaux that the children will appreciate. In the magnificent park there is a children's playground, petting zoo and a giant labyrinth. Also has picnic areas and a restaurant.
Tel: 02 54 00 10 66. www.chateau-valencay.com. Open: daily. Admission charge.

Le Clos Lucé

Leonardo da Vinci's house at Le Clos Lucé has collections of his fabulous machines and scale models of his inventions for kids to try out.
2 rue de Clos Lucé. Tel: 02 47 57 00 73. www.vinci-closluce.com. Open: daily. Admission charge.

Les Cerqueux-sous-Passavant

Bisonland is a game park where deer and bison are bred in the grounds of the **Château des Landes**. Dried bison, bison sausages and pâté are also sold.

25km (15 miles) south of Angers. Tel: 02 41 59 58 02. Open: May–mid-Sept daily; rest of year Sun & holiday afternoons. Admission charge.

Doué-la-Fontaine

The **Zoo de Doué**, one of the best in Europe, uses caverns and quarries to house some 500 endangered species in near-natural surroundings. Cafeteria.
17km (10 miles) southwest of Saumur. Tel: 02 41 59 18 58. www.zoodoue.fr. Open: Feb–Oct daily. Admission charge.

La Flèche

In addition to the 800 wild animals, such as the hippopotamus, giraffe and leopard, local species are also on view in the **Parc Zoologique du Tetre Rouge**, which also has a museum of natural history featuring 600 stuffed animals.
50km (31 miles) northeast of Angers. Tel: 02 43 48 19 19. www.zoo-la-fleche.com. Open: daily. Admission charge.

Haute-Touche

Rare species, such as the European wolf, are among the 1,000 animals roaming

Making friends at the Château de Valencay petting zoo

freely in the **Haute-Touche Wildlife Park**. *3km (2 miles) north of Azay-le-Ferron. Tel: 02 54 02 20 40. Open: Easter–mid-Nov daily. Admission charge.*

Lussault de Tourain

This is the largest aquarium of freshwater fish in Europe with over 10,000 fish, 54 tanks, a shark tunnel and an open tank where fish can be stroked. *3km (2 miles) from Amboise. Tel: 02 47 23 44 57. www.aquariumduvaldeloire.com. Open: daily. Admission charge.*

Nantes

What was once swampland has been transformed into an oriental garden, animated with waterfalls and rockeries and planted with exotic plants. The **Maison d l'Erdre** presents local fauna and flora and houses an aquarium. *Ile de Versailles. Tel: 02 40 29 41 11. Open: Wed–Mon. Admission charge.*

Musée de Jules Verne

Jules Verne was born in Nantes and this museum dedicated to him has three floors of objects and mementos – books, manuscripts, games and photos. *3 rue de l'Hermitage. Tel: 02 40 69 72 52. Open: Wed–Mon. Closed: Sun morning. Admission charge.*

Nyoiseau-Châtelais

The **Domaine de la Petite Couère** is a vast 80ha (197-acre) park, with paths linking display areas for animals (from llamas to emus), a collection of old farm

vehicles, old cars (rather ordinary), old shops (grocers) and homes – all trying to show life as it was a century ago. Quite fun for small children, with room to run free. *Near Segré, 35km (21 miles) northwest of Angers. Tel: 02 41 61 06 31. Open: Apr–Nov Tue–Sun. Admission charge.*

Saint-Aignan-sur-Cher

The **Zoo Parc de Beauval** has white tigers among its 30 big cats, plus 100 monkeys on an island, 100 snakes and 500 exotic birds in a 12ha (29-acre) park. Picnic areas, cafeterias. *35km (21 miles) south of Blois. Tel: 02 54 75 50 00. www.zoobeauval.com. Open: daily. Admission charge.*

Saint-Hilaire-Saint-Florent

Displays by the Cadre Noir, competitions and guided tours of the stables make the **École Nationale d'Equitation** (National Riding School) a must for fans of the horse (*see pp48–9*).

Excellent aquariums at Lussault and Nantes reveal the secrets of life underwater

At Terrefort, above St-Hilaire-St-Florent.
Tel: 02 41 53 50 60. www.cadrenoir.fr.
Open: Apr–Sept daily. Closed: Sun, Mon
& Sat afternoons. Admission charge.

Mushrooms are the subject of the
Musée du Champignon, la Houssaye –
cultivated in an old tufa quarry.
Tel: 02 41 50 31 55. www.musee-du-
champignon.com. Open: mid-Feb–mid-
Nov daily. Admission charge.

Saint-Mathurin-sur-Loire

Learn how the Loire River has been
controlled over the centuries in the
Observatoire de la Vallée d'Anjou,
located in a former railway station.
20km (12 miles) east of Angers.
Tel: 02 41 57 08 18. Open: Apr–Oct
Sat & Sun, Jul & Aug Tue–Sun.
Admission charge.

Saint-Sylvain-d'Anjou

The precursors of the elegant Loire
châteaux are represented here by the
reconstructed 12th-century motte-and-
bailey Château à Motte in the **Parc de
la Haie Joulain.**
5km (3 miles) northeast of Angers.
Tel: 02 41 76 81 78. Open: Jun–Aug
daily. Admission charge.

Saumur

At the **Musée des Blindés** is one of the
world's finest collections of military
tanks from more than a dozen
countries, many still in working order.
Rue Fricotelle. Tel: 02 41 83 69 95.
www.museedesblindes.fr.
Open: daily. Admission charge.

The **Musée de la Cavalerie** traces the
deeds of the French cavalry since the
18th century.
Tel: 02 41 83 69 23. www.
museecavalerie.free.fr. Open: Mon–Thur,
Sat–Sun pm. Admission charge.

Spay

Some 250 species of exotic birds
wander freely in the **Jardin des
Oiseaux**. Picnic areas.
10km (6 miles) south of Le Mans.
Tel: 02 43 21 33 02. www.zoospay.com.
Open: daily. Admission charge.

Tours

The **Musée du Compagnonnage**
celebrates the centuries-old guilds of
craftsmen. The masterpieces on show
range from embroidered white satin
slippers dating from 1837 to a gold-
medal winner of 1934 – a scale model
of Milan's cathedral.
Clôitre St-Julien, 8 rue Nationale.
Tel: 02 47 21 62 20. Open: Jun–Sept
daily, Oct–May Wed–Mon.
Admission charge.

Trélazé

The **Musée de l'Ardoise** is one of
several in the region dedicated to the
history of slate-quarrying. Good
demonstrations.
5km (3 miles) southeast of Angers,
32 rue de la Maraîchère. Tel: 02 41 69
04 71. Open: mid-Feb–Jun & mid-
Sept–Nov Sat & Sun pm, Jul–mid-Sept
Tue–Sun pm. Closed: Mon.
Admission charge.

Sport and leisure

Endowed with beautiful scenery, the Loire Valley's sporting attractions are focused on the outdoors. The landscape combines the old world charm of châteaux with rolling greens, rivers and streams – all never too far away.

GOLF

The Loire Valley has many courses, including some quite testing ones (*see www.golflounge.com*). The settings are attractive and some courses are situated in the grounds of a château. For a full list of the ever-growing number of clubs, contact the Fédération française de golf, *www.ffgolf.org*

Golf Club d'Angers

This attractive, par-70 course has plenty of water hazards.
5km (3 miles) southeast of Angers at Brissac-Quincé. Tel: 02 41 91 96 56.

Anjou Golf and Country Club

Designed by the well-known Fred Hawtree, this 18-hole, par-72 course is one of the longest in the region at 6,250m (6,835yds).
20km north of Angers off the A11. Tel: 02 41 42 01 01.

Ardrée-Tours Golf Club

A pleasant course in the heart of the country with a château in the background. Giant cedars line the broad fairways; par 72.
12km (7 miles) north of Tours, at Château d'Ardrée, St-Antoine-du-Rocher. Tel: 02 47 56 77 38.

Geography and climate create perfect golfing conditions

Les Bordes International Golf Club

Built with money from Baron Bic (of ball point pen and razor fame) and designed by Robert von Hagge, this 18-hole monster, with a par of 72, is one of France's finest.

30km southwest of Orléans, at St-Laurent-Nouan. Tel: 02 54 87 72 13.

Château des Sept Tours Golf Club

Although flat and easy to walk, the architects, Pete and Don Harradine, have used lakes on eight of the holes to test golfers.

35km (21 miles) west of Tours, at Courcelles-de-Touraine.
Tel: 02 47 24 69 75.

Cheverny Golf Club

The Château de Cheverny is the centre-piece for the course (which opened in 1989), a challenging 6,273m (6,850yds) long with a par of 71. There is plenty of water to negotiate.

13km south of Blois. Tel: 02 54 79 24 70.

Cholet Golf Club

A tricky mixture of water hazards and dog legs; 18 holes, par 71.

58km southwest of Angers, near town centre, allée du Chêne Landry.
Tel: 02 41 71 05 01.

L'Epinay Golf Course

Martin Hawtree designed this pleasant 18-hole resort course which, at 5,790m (6,332yds), is not too testing.

5km (3 miles) northeast of Nantes. Take the RN23 towards Angers, then Carquefou. Tel: 02 40 52 73 74.

Golf Club du Mans

In the middle of the 24-hour motor-racing circuit, with plenty of pine trees and heather, this is a well-established course; 18 holes, par 71.

Just south of Le Mans, Route de Tours. Tel: 02 43 42 00 36.

Golf de Marcilly-en-Villette

An 18-hole course, 20km (12 miles) southeast of Orléans at Domaine de la Plaine.

Tel: 02 38 76 11 73.

Golf de Nantes-Erdre

A quiet parkland course outside Nantes; 18 holes, par 71.

Just northwest of the city on the Rennes road (RN137). Tel: 02 40 59 21 21.

Touraine Golf Club

One of the easiest, but also one of the oldest, courses in the Loire Valley; 5,730m (6,266yds), par 71. The clubhouse is in the Château de la Touche.

5km (3 miles) southwest of Tours, near Ballan-Miré. Tel: 02 47 53 20 28.

FISHING

The French are mad about both game and coarse fishing. Although different regions have slightly different regulations, there are two basic river categories or classifications. *Première catégorie* rivers, open from about March to September, are for game fishing (trout and salmon); *deuxième catégorie* streams, open almost all year long, are for coarse fishing. In the Loire and its numerous tributaries the main prize is the *brochet* (pike). Also popular are *sandre* (zander or pike-perch), *perche* (perch), *gardon* (roach), *carpe* (carp), *brème* (bream), *goujon* (gudgeon) and *anguille* (eel).

Sport and leisure

All you need is time, patience, a licence . . . and lots of luck

Each *département* issues its own licences (which are mandatory), and this can make life difficult for the casual angler. Fortunately, several hotels and tour operators cater to anglers. A useful map is *Pêche en France* (Fishing in France) prepared by the **Conseil Supérieur de la Pêche** (*16 ave Louison Bobet, 94132 Fontenay-sous-Bois; tel: 01 45 14 36 00; www.csp.environnement. gouv.fr*). Also available at tourist offices.

LEISURE PARKS

When children want to stop sightseeing, *centres de loisirs* (leisure parks) are ideal places to visit. The following are the locations of the bigger ones.

Angers

Parc de Loisirs du Lac de Maine has everything from windsurfers and canoes to tennis and a café.
49 avenue du Lac de Maine. Tel: 02 41 22 32 10.

Chalonnes-sur-Loire

Les Goulidons is a peaceful setting for fishing, mountain-bike hire, horse-riding and tennis.
20km (12 miles) southwest of Angers. Tel: 02 41 78 03 58.

Cholet

Centre d'Initiation aux Sports de Plein Air is a centre with camp site, canoes, mountain bikes, horses and tennis.
Port de Ribou, 58km (36 miles) southwest of Angers. Tel: 02 41 49 80 60.

Couture-sur-le-Loir

The **Trois Lacs** leisure centre has jet-skis and 4-wheeled bikes.
45km (28 miles) north of Tours. Tel: 02 41 95 44 75.

Mansigné

A vast stretch of water great for sailing, and for riding and biking on the shore; there is also an indoor heated swimming pool, welcome during spring and autumn holidays.
60km (37 miles) northeast of Angers. Tel: 02 43 46 14 17.

Marçon

The **Marçon Centre de Loisirs** offers boats and surfboards for hire, plus tennis and horse riding.
40km (25 miles) northwest of Tours, near Château-du-Loir. Tel: 02 43 44 13 07.

Nantes

The **Centre de Loisirs de Petit Port** complex has two swimming pools, an

ice-skating rink (of Olympic proportions), a bowling alley and billiard rooms.
Blvd de Petit Port. Tel: 02 51 84 94 51.

Noyant-la-Grayère

Parc de Loisirs Saint-Blaise offers well-supervised swimming, canoes and horseriding, plus a campsite.
36km (22 miles) northwest of Angers. Tel: 02 41 61 75 39.

La Possonnière

The **Arche** amusement and leisure park has waterslides as well as pedaloes and swimming.
On the Route de St-Georges-sur-Loire, 15km (9 miles) southwest of Angers. Tel: 02 41 72 21 09.

AERIAL SPORTS

Association Sportive de Vol à Voile
There is a gliding school that also organises short flights for the visitor to discover the region from the air.
At Angers airport. Route de Chaumont Marcé. Tel: 02 41 33 50 62.

ULM Club Val de Loire
This microlight club has a special circuit that includes a tour of the château from the air.
10km (6 miles) from Sully sur Loire. St Benoit sur Loire. Tel: 02 38 35 76 78.

WATERSPORTS

Canoe-Kayak Club de Tours
Beginners' lessons given, as well as hourly, daily or weekly escapades on the river for the more experienced.

Quai Georges Vallerey, Tours. Tel: 02 47 44 92 66.

Canoe Kayak Club Orléans
A canoe club with a difference. Discover both the flora and fauna of the Loire River on organised outings with a guide.
Base Ile de Charlemagne, 8 km (5 miles) from Orléans, Saint-Jean-le-Banc. Tel: 02 38 66 14 80.

Touraine Surf Voile
Windsurfing club on Lake Peupleraies outside Tours. Not suitable for children younger than seven years old.
Tel: 02 47 44 41 33.

OTHER SPORTS

Mini Racing Team Brosse Mouline
Choose your method – hire a crosscar, trial bike or hovercraft and take a turn around the track.
Luzillé, 10km (6 miles) south of Chenonceaux. Tel: 02 47 30 20 07.

Centre Hippique des Trois Provinces
By the hour or the day, take a pony or horse ride.
Getigné, 4km (2½ miles) from Clisson. Tel: 02 40 54 28 52.

Families swim in the Vienne

Food and drink

André Curnonsky (1872–1956), the food writer born in Angers, praised la mesure *(the moderation) of the Loire Valley cuisine, where ingredients are allowed 'to taste of what they are.' This 'garden of France', as the 16th-century writer Rabelais called it, produces everything for the kitchen: tender vegetables and fruits; fish from the Loire and nearby Atlantic Ocean; veal, pork and lamb from north of the river; and wild boar, venison, pheasant and wild mushrooms from the Sologne.*

OPENING HOURS

Restaurant opening hours are fairly standard throughout the region, with lunch available from 12 or 12.30pm until 2pm and evening meals served from around 7.30pm to 9 or 9.30pm. Usually there is a choice of good value set-price menus of two to five courses

Cheese and wine go well together

BEURRE BLANC

This is the famous sauce used to accompany fish.
Beware: it is not as simple as it looks – patience is the key.

Ingredients
3 shallots, chopped as finely as possible;
3 tablespoons white wine;
3 tablespoons white wine vinegar;
250g (9oz) unsalted butter;
salt and freshly ground black pepper.

Method
Simmer the shallots with the wine and white wine vinegar in a heavy-based pan until well reduced and thick. Allow to cool (this can be done ahead of time). Use a whisk to add the butter, a knob at a time, over a very low heat. The mixture should slowly turn into a thick creamy sauce.

The Trick
Take the pan off the heat repeatedly during whisking so the butter does not overheat.

Set menus are a great option for meals

at a range of reasonable prices. These are posted by the entrance so you can check them out before coming into the restaurant. If you are vegetarian, stress this to the waiter as some chefs consider fish or even lardons as acceptable vegetarian fare. At the end of the meal, in most places there is a service charge included in the bill.

FOOD

There is no such thing as a traditional 'Loire Valley' style of food as the region doesn't really exist in a meaningful sense. The closest thing to a regional dish is *sandre au beurre blanc* (pike-perch in a white wine sauce) or *friture de la Loire* (small fried whitebait-style fish). Instead there are lots of localised specialities connected to individual towns. In general, though, the region

nicknamed 'the garden of France' boasts a superb range of foodstuffs to choose from.

As you'd imagine, there is some great freshwater fish to eat while travelling along the Loire River. Pike-perch, shad and tench are all readily available, as are lamprey and eels. Game is also widespread, with deer, hare and wild boar appearing on menus along with pheasant and partridge. Charcuterie is popular and particularly tasty: look out for *rillettes*, shredded and potted slow-cooked pork, particularly in Tours. *Rillons*, chunks of crunchy, fried salted pork belly, aren't for the faint-hearted or vegetarian but taste delicious. The countryside supports a wealth of salad vegetables as well as flavourful peas, radishes, turnips, leeks and carrots.

(*Cont. on p164*)

Menu reader

agneau	lamb
ail	garlic
alose	shad (fish)
andouilles, andouillettes	sausages made from pig's intestines and herbs
anguille (en matelote)	eel (stewed in red wine)
artichauts (à la vinaigrette)	artichokes (cold, with an oil and vinegar dressing)
asperges	asparagus
barboille, poulet en	chicken stew, a Berry speciality
basilique	basil
beurre blanc	white sauce (usually served with fish – see p160)
biftek	beefsteak
boeuf	beef
boudins blancs	white sausage
boudins noirs	blood sausage (black pudding)
bouilleture	fish stewed in red wine
broche, à la	on a spit
brochet (à l'orléanaise)	pike (Orléans-style, baked with a vinegar and shallot sauce)
brochette, en	kebab-style
cailles	quails
canards, canetons	duck, duckling
carpe	carp
cèpes	boletus mushrooms
cerf	red deer (stag)
cervelle	brains
champignons	mushrooms
chanciot	Berry speciality of apple batter dessert
chanterelles	wild mushrooms
Chavignol	goat's cheese; served grilled with a salad

chèvre	goat
chevreuil	venison (technically roe deer)
chou	cabbage
choufleur	cauliflower
crémet or coeurs à la crème	a mixture of cream, cream cheese and egg white, often eaten with fresh berries
cresson	cress
crottins	goat's cheese in balls
daim	fallow deer
darne de saumon	salmon steak
dinde/ dindonneau	turkey
eau (gazeuse, plate)	water (sparkling, flat)
épinards	spinach
escargots	snails
estragon	tarragon
faisan	pheasant
farci	stuffed
fenouil	fennel
foie	liver
fonds d'artichauts	artichoke hearts
fouaces	bread rolls, traditionally baked in a wood-fired oven
four, au	in the oven
fraises	strawberries
framboises	raspberries
fricassée de poulet à l'angevine	chicken, onions and mushrooms simmered in dry white wine and served with cream
frit	fried
frites	chips, french-fried potatoes

fumé	smoked	**pruneau**	prune
girolles	a type of wild mushroom	**quenelles de brochet**	poached pike dumplings
grenouille	frog	**rillettes**	potted meat (usually pork, sometimes goose)
haricots	beans		
jambon	ham		
lapin, lapereau	rabbit		
lièvre	hare	**romarin**	rosemary
marcassin	young boar	**sanglier**	wild boar
marrons	sweet chestnuts	**saucisse**	fresh sausage, which has to be cooked, as opposed to saucisson, a dried or smoked sausage, ready to eat
matelote	fish or eel stew with red wine		
morilles	wild mushrooms (morels)		
mûres	blackberries	**saumon (à l'oseille)**	salmon (with sorrel)
myrtilles	blueberries		
noisettes de porc aux pruneaux de Tours	pork with prunes	**Selles-sur-Cher**	goat's cheese
		steak Curnonsky	named after the Loire's famous food writer: fillets of beef with beef marrow and grilled tomatoes, port and brandy sauce
nouilles	noodles		
oeufs pochés à la mode d'Orléans	poached eggs on small chicken tarts with a sauce suprême (cream sauce)		
		steak à la tourangelle	fillets of beef with foie-gras-stuffed prunes and Madeira sauce
oie	goose		
Olivet	flat disk of cow's milk cheese from Orléans	**Sainte-Maure**	cylindrical goats' cheese with straw running through it
omelette (aux fine herbes)	omelettes (with chopped herbs)		
oseille	sorrel	**Tarte Tatin**	apple tart (*see page 100*)
perche	perch		
persil	parsley	**Valençay**	pyramidal goat's cheese
petite friture de la Loire	deep-fried assortment of freshwater fish		
pigeon, pigeonneux (crapaudine)	pigeon (spatchcocked and grilled)	**veau (cul de)**	veal (rump)
		venaison	venison
pintade, pintadeau	guinea fowl		
porc	pork		
potage (à la tourangelle)	soup (Tours-style with chicken, cabbage, peas, leeks and turnips)		
poulet	chicken		
prune	plum		

Samphire thrives on the salt marshes near Nantes and asparagus can be found around Sologne. Mushrooms are cultivated in damp caves and hollows. There is also good fruit to be found, with apples and pears popular around Angers and sumptuous strawberries coming from Saumur, while Tours is well-known for its prunes, often served steeped in wine or with pork. Tours is also the place to try *fouaces* or *fouées*, wheat bread fast-cooked in hot oven embers and usually stuffed with cheese or *rillons* then served with various dipping sauces.

WHAT TO EAT

Soups are simple: *potage à la tourangelle* is based on chicken broth, dotted with the excellent young peas, turnips, leeks and cabbages of the area. *Bouilleture* is

Troglodyte caves make for cozy restaurants

a thick soup or stew of freshwater fish with wine; *matelote* is an eel stew using red wine. More delicate are the *quenelles de brochet* (ovals of poached pike mousse).

Among main dishes, one of the best known is *noisettes de porc aux pruneaux de Tours* (pork medallions cooked with prunes), while *fricassée de poulet à l'angevine* combines chicken with onions and mushrooms in white wine and cream.

In summer, a typical dessert could be *crémets* (cream, cream cheese and egg beaten together) served with fresh strawberries or raspberries. The most famous dish of the region, however, is the legendary *Tarte Tatin* (*see p100*), a caramelly apple tart. Purists are shocked by the (delicious) variation that uses pears. Cakes and confectionery also appear as desserts, with regional specialities on offer: in Tours try Nougat de Tours, in Angers Quernon d'Ardoise (nougat-stuffed square of chocolate) and in Orléans the highly concentrated quince jelly Cotignacs d'Orléans.

Most of the cheeses that are produced in the region are made from goat's milk. They are delicious, so don't be put off by the names. The *crottin de Chavignol* is a small, dry cheese that resembles horse dung (*crottin* in French). Sainte-Maure is recognised by the straw threaded through the cheese, while Valençay is pyramidal. The best-known cow's milk cheese is the *olivet*, from Orléans.

WHERE TO EAT

The following symbols indicate the price per person of a three course meal with a half bottle of wine:

£ under €25
££ €25–35
£££ €35–50
££££ over €50

THE WESTERN LOIRE

Angers

Le Favre d'Anne £££–££££
This Michelin-starred restaurant is located in a smart house with beautiful views across the garden and river to the château, dishing up seasonal menus of refined, modern food alongside a list of local wines.
18 quai des Larmes.
Tel: 02 41 36 12 12.

La Ferme £££–££££
Close to the cathedral and featuring a frequently heaving outdoor terrace, this rustic dining room decked out in farming memorabilia serves up traditional dishes such as pot-au-feu and cassoulets, with ingredients sourced locally.

2 place Frepper.
Tel: 02 41 87 09 90.

Chenillé-Changé
Le Table du Meunier £££
A converted mill on the river where the setting enhances the straightforward food. There is a large range of ciders on offer alongside the Anjou wines here.
In the centre of Chenillé-Changé.
Tel: 02 41 95 10 98.

Clisson
La Bonne Auberge £££
Amazing things are done with lobster in this stylish eaterie, which also serves up delicate desserts.
1 rue Olivier-de-Clisson.
Tel: 02 40 54 01 90.

Courçay
La Couture ££
The sort of country inn that visitors look for; situated in a fortified farmhouse.
On the RN 143.
Tel: 02 47 94 16 44.

Doué-La-Fontaine
Auberge de Bienvenue ££
Pretty auberge serving up a cosy atmosphere

and well-chosen produce.
104 route de Cholet.
Tel: 02 41 59 22 44.

La Flèche
Moulin des Quatre Saison £££
Great-looking seventeenth century mill that has been converted into a sophisticated restaurant.
rue Galliens.
Tel: 02 43 45 12 12.

Montsoreau
Diane de Méridor ££
While dining, check out both the views of the river and the château. Specialises in freshwater fish dishes.
12 quai Philippe de Commines.
Tel: 02 41 51 71 76.

Nantes
Crêperie Heb-Ken ££
A vast array of savoury *galettes* and sweet crêpes are on offer in this authentic Breton crêperie, serving a range of ciders with which to wash them down.
5 rue de Guérande.
Tel: 02 40 48 79 07.

La Cigale £££

A large selection of high quality brasserie dishes using superior ingredients are served up in this swish *belle époque* Monument Historique dating from 1895.
4 place Graslin.
Tel: 02 51 84 94 94.

L'Atlantide £££–££££

Rooftop views are on offer at this exclusive restaurant where innovative contemporary dishes and a well-chosen wine list are available.
16 quai Ernest-Renaud.
Tel: 02 40 73 23 23.

Onzain

Domaine des Hauts de Loire ££££

The restaurant in this grand hunting pavilion enjoys a superb setting. Expensive but refined regional cuisine worth every centime is on offer.
route d'Herbault.
Tel: 02 54 20 72 57.

St-Hilaire-St-Florent

Les Clos des Bénédictines £££

Fine views over the city and well-prepared dishes.
On the D751.
Tel: 02 41 67 28 48.

Saumur

Auberge St Pierre ££–£££

Eat house specialities and regional delicacies on the terrace set in a square not far from the château.
6 place St Pierre.
Tel: 02 41 51 26 25.

L'Orangerie ££–£££

This modern brasserie dealing in regional specialities sits at the foot of the château drawbridge.
Tel: 02 41 67 12 88.

WEST CENTRAL LOIRE

Tours

Café du Vieux Mûrier ££

This is the best of the bar-restaurants on vibrant Place 'Plum', named after the mulberry tree out the front under which people shelter while watching the world go by.
11 place Plumereau.
Tel: 02 47 61 04 77.

Comme Autrefouée ££

Traditional dough balls stuffed with various fillings are available in this informal restaurant.
11 rue de la Monnaie.
Tel: 02 47 05 94 78.

Bistrot de la Tranchée ££–£££

Try this bistro by the same team behind Barrier, next door, which does great dishes at more affordable prices.
103 av de la Tranchée.
Tel: 02 47 41 09 08.

Charles Barrier ££££

The grand old man of Tour's cuisine has been operating on the north bank for more than 50 years, producing exceptional, inventive, frequently changing menus.
101 av de la Tranchée.
Tel: 02 47 54 20 39.

Amboise

Bigot £

This award-winning salon de thé serves patisseries, macaroons, cakes and delicious chocolatey treats alongside salads, omelettes and savoury flans.
place du Château.
Tel: 02 47 57 04 46.

Chez Bruno ££

This small, atmospheric bistro with château views from its terrace, boasts good value food and an exceptional local wine list.
place du Château.
Tel: 02 47 57 73 49.

L'Épicerie £££

The Grocery, set in an historical timber-framed

house beneath the château, has attractive neo-Renaissance décor and a classic menu of hearty regional fare.
46 place Debré.
Tel: 02 47 57 08 94.

Azay-Le-Rideau
L'Aigle d'Or ££
The best bet in this busy touristy town. Food is unimaginative but reliably rendered.
10 rue A-Riché.
Tel: 02 47 45 24 58.

Chinon
Les Années 30 ££–£££
A stylish small restaurant in the old quarter that has a tempting selection of menus that are both reasonably priced and just a little bit different from the norm.
78 rue Voltaire,
Tel: 02 47 93 37 18.
Le Chapeau Rouge £££
Well located on an attractive square, this decent brasserie is the place to sample Chinon wines alongside their tasty main meals.
49 place du Général de Gaulle.
Tel: 02 47 98 08 08.

Fontevraud
La Licorne £££–££££
Next to the abbey in an 18th-century house complete with courtyard and elegant dining room is this traditional restaurant with a strong reputation for tasty food and Saumur wines.
Allée St Catherine.
Tel: 02 41 51 72 49.

Loches
Auberge Le Vilariat ££
A good value eaterie, actually in the citadel, where waiters in medieval costume serve up recreations of old recipes.
4 place Charles VII.
Tel: 02 47 59 08 79.
Le George-Sand £££
Below the ramparts of the château, overlooking a weir, this competent restaurant also has an attractive terrace.
39 rue Quintefol.
Tel: 02 47 59 39 74.

Luynes
Domaine de Beauvois ££££
You'll find elegant dining in this countryside château.
D49, northwest.
Tel: 02 47 55 50 11.

Montbazon
La Chancelière ££££
The affluent citizens of Tours come to this elegant old house in the centre of Montbazon when they want to celebrate with uncomplicated but exceptionally cooked modern cuisine.
1 place Montbazon.
Tel: 02 47 26 00 67.
Château d'Artigny ££££
One of the most splendid hotel dining rooms in the region, this is both upmarket and expensive.
route d'Azay-le-Rideau.
Tel: 02 47 34 30 30.

Montoire Sur Le Loire
Le Cheval Rouge £
Classic French cooking is found here – not far from Trôo and Lavardin.
place Foch.
Tel: 02 54 85 07 05.

Saché
Auberge de XIIe Siecle £££
This characteristic inn with a fabulous fireplace serves flavoursome, classic dishes using carefully chosen local ingredients and offers good wine too.

1 rue de Château.
Tel: 02 47 26 88 77.

Rochecorbon
L'Oubliette ££–£££
Classy cooking tucked
away in a troglodyte
cave.
34 rue Clouets.
Tel: 02 47 52 50 49.
Les Hautes Roches ££££
Perched on a cliff side,
this luxurious restaurant
attached to a hotel serves
Michelin-starred cuisine
at correspondingly high
rates.
86 quai de la Loire.
Tel: 02 47 52 88 88.

Thouracé
**Le Relais de
Bonnezeaux ££**
Delicate dishes and
Layon wines are served
in this converted station.
route Angers.
Tel: 02 41 54 08 33.

Villandry
**Domaine de la
Giraudière £££**
All the food is home-
made at this charming
17th-century farmhouse
restaurant, which draws
heavily from its herds of
goats for delicious cheeses
and desserts.

route de Druye.
Tel: 02 47 50 08 60.
L'Etape Gourmande £££
The rustic cooking at this
working 17th-century
courtyard farm is well-
conceived and executed,
and uses produce from
the farm itself.
*Domaine de la
Giraudière.*
Tel: 02 47 50 08 60.

Vouvray
La Cave Martin ££
Here is your chance to
eat honest rustic dishes
in a real cave, and sample
local wines.
66 La Vallée Coquette.
Tel: 20 47 52 62 18.

Vignoux-Sur-
Barrangeon
Le Prieuré ££££
Discover serious fish
cookery off the beaten
track at this venerable
hotel restaurant in a
former priory.
*route St-Laurent, on the
D30. Tel: 02 48 51 58 80.*

EAST CENTRAL LOIRE
Orléans
A Bon Marché ££
In the heart of Old
Orléans is this typically
French restaurant-cum-

wine shop that has
a range of superb
regional dishes and
a great selection of
local wines.
12 place de Châtelet.
Tel: 02 38 53 03 35.
Le Brin de Zinc ££
This large, lively
brasserie on a back
street off place Martroi
has a wide-ranging
menu from mussels
and seafood to game
and bistro staples,
all at reasonable
rates.
62 rue St Catherine,
Tel: 02 38 53 38 77.
**Orléans La Chancellerie
££–£££**
An efficient brasserie in a
splendid building on the
main square.
27 place du Martroi.
Tel: 02 38 53 57 54.
Le Lift £££
The chef at this modern,
contemporary bistro
with an ideally situated
terrace overlooking
the Loire, cooks
creative versions of
traditional dishes,
drawing heavily on
seasonal and regional
influences.
place de la Loire.
Tel: 02 38 53 63 48.

Blois

Les Banquettes Rouges ££

This relaxed, hip little bistro in Old Blois offers up delicious and generous portions of local favourites.
126 rue des Trois Marchands.
Tel: 02 54 78 74 92.

Le Castelet ££

If you are looking for good value menus based around filling, fresh, locally sourced produce then this cosy restaurant decorated with murals will fit the bill.
40 rue St Lubin.
Tel: 02 54 74 66 09.

Au Rendez-vous des Pécheurs £££

This celebrated local bistro focuses on freshly caught fish and seasonal vegetables but also has a good selection of rustic dishes.
27 rue du Foix.
Tel: 02 54 74 67 48.

L'Orangerie ££££

Situated in the château's fifteenth-century former winter garden, the sumptuous setting is matched by the haute cuisine and regional specialities on offer. Indulgent and expensive but worth treating yourself.
1 avenue Jean Laigret.
Tel: 02 54 78 05 36.

Souvigny-en-Sologne

Le Perdrix Rouge ££

Jean-Noël Beurienne is famous for his seasonal Sologne game dishes. The food is always excellent.
rue Gâtinais.
Tel: 02 54 88 41 05.

Vendome

Le Petit Bilboquet ££

Regional dishes but a delight awaits those with a sweet tooth.
Ancienne Route des Tours.
Tel: 02 54 77 16 60.

THE EASTERN LOIRE

Bourges

Le Bourbonnoux ££

Chic, rather fancy modern cooking that is well worth a visit.
44 rue Bourbonnoux.
Tel: 02 48 24 14 76.

La Courcilliere ££

Situated by the marshes, this restaurant specialises in freshwater fish but also has surprises such as lentil ice cream on offer.
rue de Babylone.
Tel: 02 48 24 41 91.

D'Antan Sancerrois ££–£££

Atmospheric bistro in a white stone dining room that serves up tasty traditional local dishes.
50 rue Bourbonnoux.
Tel: 02 48 65 96 26.

Gien

Restaurant La Poularde £££

Smart bistro on the banks of the Loire that has a tasteful dining room kitted out with Gien tableware. Menus include fish and game when in season.
13 quai de Nice.
Tel: 02 38 67 36 05.

Sancerre

Auberge Le Pomme d'Or ££

Cosy restaurant in a former coaching inn that offers basic, uncomplicated dishes – and it does so very well – letting local flavours dominate.
place de la Mairie.
Tel: 02 48 54 13 30.

Loire Valley wines

The sheer diversity of Loire wines comes as a surprise to many visitors. The choice includes red, white and rosé, dry, medium and sweet, and even *pétillant* (sparkling). The wines range from crisp, appley whites to full-bodied reds. Often served by the glass (12cl), the *fillette* (a pitcher of 25cl) or the *chopine* (50cl).

Muscadet

Made from the Melon de Bourgogne grape, this is the standard accompaniment to a platter of *fruits de mer*. The better Muscadets are from Sèvre-et-Maine, labelled 'sur lie', meaning that the pressed juice is left throughout the winter on the lees in the vat before bottling in the spring: this gives a fuller flavour and adds zing to this light, crisp wine.

From the same area, around Nantes, the Folle Blanche grape is used to make the very acidic Gros Plant white wine.

Anjou and Saumur

Anjou is best known internationally for the mass-market sales of its sweetish pink Anjou Rosé. Wine experts, however, rave about the dry white Savennières, made just west of

Wine from every vineyard has its own particular flavour

GRANDS VINS DE VOUVRAY

Vouvray wines can be still or sparkling, sweet or dry

Angers from Chenin Blanc grapes, which are at their best after a decade in the bottle. Challenging Champagne in popularity are the sparkling Saumur *brut* (dry) sparkling wines, some even owned by Champagne houses. The Cabernet Franc grape is grown for light quaffable red wines, such as Saumur Rouge and Saumur-Champigny, often drunk chilled in summer.

Touraine

The Cabernet Franc seems to have more character and depth of flavour further upstream around Chinon, Bourgeuil and Saint-Nicholas-de-Bourgeuil. When allowed to mature, their complexity approaches that of fine Burgundies.

Around Vouvray and Montlouis, the Chenin Blanc grape is transformed into classy dry, *demi-sec* (medium dry), sweet and *mousseux* (sparkling) white wines. When it comes to value

for money, try the refreshing Sauvignon de Touraine, a clean-tasting white wine that is a particular pleasure to drink in summer.

Sancerre and Pouilly-Fumé

Until New Zealand came along, no place in the world produced finer Sauvignon Blanc wines than the eastern extremes of the Loire vineyards, with their leafy freshness and elegant balance.

Other wines

Hidden away in the Layon Valley are the well-priced dessert wines of the Côteaux du Layon. On the Loir, locals are fiercely proud of their unusual Jasnières (pronounced 'Jannyair'). Near Bourges, the Sauvignon Blanc and Pinot Gris grapes make Quincy, Reuilly and Menetou-Salon wines; these dry whites and light reds are less expensive than similar Sancerres.

Accommodation

Visitors are nothing new in the Loire Valley. Back in 1539, Charles V of Spain was the guest of François I at Chambord. Today, you don't have to be royalty to stay in a château; many have been transformed into hotels, ranging from the grand Château d'Artigny near Tours to the smaller Château de Beaulieu at Joué-lès-Tours.

Unless you are travelling during July, August or early September, it is rarely difficult to find a room at the price and standard you require. During the summer holidays, however, advance reservations are essential.

The star-rating system

There are five grades of hotels in France: 1-, 2-, 3- and 4-star, and the 4-star *luxe* (luxury) category. These stars

Star ratings in the signage are an indication of the facilities on offer

reflect the range of facilities rather than quality, so a comfortable and friendly 2-star hotel may be more to your liking than a more formal 4-star hotel which has porters, receptionists and a swimming pool.

The French Government Tourist Office (often known as La Maison de la France) has branches all over the world, where full listings of hotels in the Loire Valley are available, as well as suggestions on how to book ahead. Their annual magazine, *The Traveller in France Reference Guide*, published in Britain, has hundreds of hotel listings, along with reservation numbers. Among the most widespread and popular hotel associations are:

Logis de France: this consists of some 4,000 family-run hotels, mainly in the 1- and 2-star category. Members are listed in a book, entitled *Logis de France*, that is published annually in March. *Tel: 01 45 84 83 84.* *www.logis-de-france.fr*

Relais & Châteaux: 400 luxury hotels, often in old castles or country mansions.
Tel: 08 25 32 32 32.
www.relaischateaux.com

Campanile: 395 modern, motel-style hotels across France.
Tel: (020) 8569 6969 (UK); 01 64 62 46 46 (France). www.campanile.fr

Atmospheric little inns dot the region

Ibis-Arcade: 400 modern hotels at 2-star level, all over France.
Tel: (020) 7724 1000 (UK); 01 60 87 90 90 (France). www.ibishotel.com

Première Classe: The ultimate economy hotel. Plain, cheap and clean rooms with bathrooms.
Tel: 08 36 68 81 23.
www.premiereclasse.fr

Once in France, it is well worth stopping at an Office de Tourisme or Syndicat d'Initiative (tourist office) for further suggestions. Some will even be able to offer assistance with your reservations.

Chambres d'Hôtes
Increasing numbers of families offer B&B in private homes, which can be cosy, quaint or very grand. Breakfast is included in the price and may simply be the traditional coffee and bread or croissant, or could include cheeses and cold meats. Chambres d'Hôtes France have a comprehensive list.
www.chambresdhotesfrance.com

Camping
Camping is popular throughout France and even the smallest village has *un camping*. Prices start from as little as €10 per person per night but scenic locations often cost more. Only camp in officially designated sites.
www.campingfrance.com

Self-catering
Thousands of French and foreign visitors prefer to rent a cottage and cater for themselves. Select the one that suits. The nationwide **Gîtes de France** organisation lists all the available properties in a thick, yellow book. It is vital to book several months in advance since the main holiday periods are quickly booked up.
Tel: 01 49 70 75 75.
www.gites-de-France.fr

At home in a château
The Loire boasts a wide selection of luxury châteaux in spectacular settings where you can stay. Quality varies but typically they feature four-poster beds, period pieces, antique furniture and

modern amenities and levels of service. Relais & châteaux publish an annual brochure of venues that are members.

Messing about on the river

The numerous rivers and canals of the Loire region are all well-served with marinas where you can hire a *péniche*, a houseboat-like holiday boat. No permits are needed and a short on-the-spot lesson by the *loueur* (boat hire company) is enough to get you started. With beds, showers, kitchens and toilets, these may look like floating caravans, but they are spacious enough to accommodate from 2 to 16 guests (*see also p134*).

Stay underground

The central *gîtes* agency for Maine-et-Loire has several *troglogîtes* – self-catering underground homes – on its books (*see also pp150–51*).
Tel: 02 41 23 51 23.

Auberge du Centre, Chitenay, extends a warm welcome; Logis de France is another hotel grouping which promises authenticity and local cooking

Prices are for a double room in peak season without breakfast, unless stated otherwise:
£ under €50
££ €50–100
£££ €100–150
££££ over €150

THE WESTERN LOIRE
Angers
Hôtel du Mail ££
This charming, converted convent in a quiet part of town has creaky floors and period pieces as well as a generous buffet breakfast.
8 rue des Ursules.
Tel: 02 41 25 05 25.
www.hotel-du-mail.com

Nantes
Hôtel des Colonies ££
Close to the action but situated on a quiet side street, this contemporary outfit is bright and bold with artistic touches, despite the plain external appearance.
5 rue de Chapeau Rouge.
Tel: 02 40 48 79 76.
Hôtel Graslin £££
Comfortable, modern rooms are on offer in this post-war block with some Art Deco influence, which is ideally placed

near the main shopping drag.
1 rue Piron.
Tel: 02 40 69 72 91.
www.hotel-graslin.com
Hôtel La Pérouse £££
Fans of the minimalist style will appreciate this modern design hotel, kitted out by big name designers.
3 allée Duquesne.
Tel: 02 40 89 75 00.
www.hotel-laperouse.fr

Saumur
Hôtel Anne d'Anjou ££££
There is a romantic air to this graceful mansion set between the Loire and the château with its impressive frontage and high-quality interior features.
32 quai Mayaud.
Tel: 02 41 67 30 30. www.
hotel-anneanjou.com

WEST CENTRAL LOIRE
Tours
Hôtel Mondial £–££
You can choose between updated, funky attic rooms and more traditional, older ones, at this good-value, central hotel on a quiet square. Note that the reception is on the first floor, rooms

are higher and there's no lift.
3 place de la Résistance.
Tel: 02 47 05 62 68. www.
hotelmondialtours.com
L'Adresse ££
City chic is on offer at this super-stylish boutique hotel on a quiet street, with rooms in soothing shades of ivory and grey, all equipped with mod-cons and smart patinated furniture.
12 rue de la Rôtisserie.
Tel: 02 47 20 85 76.
www.hotel-ladresse.com

Amboise
Villa Mary ££–£££
Just a handful of rooms are on offer in this luxurious 18th-century town house full of period features and furniture.
14 rue de la Concorde.
Tel: 02 47 23 03 31.
www.villa-mary.fr
Le Clos d'Amboise £££
The impeccably furnished and elegantly decorated rooms here have separate seating areas, while the substantial grounds hide a swimming pool and a converted stable houses a sauna and gym.

27 rue Rabelais.
Tel: 02 47 30 10 20.
www.leclosamboise.com

Azay-le-Rideau
Hôtel de Biencourt ££
Close to the château stands this charming hotel with light, high-ceilinged rooms and a converted school building that now sleeps some of the visitors.
7 rue Balzac.
Tel: 02 47 45 20 75.
www.hotelbiencourt.com
Le Grand Monarque £££
Occupying a former post office and a grand house, this hotel has exposed brickwork, wooden beams and is decorated stylishly with rustic furniture and antiques. Lunch can be taken on a private terrace or in the well-presented dining room.
3 place de la République.
Tel: 02 47 45 40 08. www.
legrandmonarque.com

Chaumont
Château de Chissay £££
Close to Montrichard and Chenonceaux, this pale tuffeau stone building provides a grand base from which to explore the

surrounding sites. There's a Gothic-style restaurant with arched vaults in the building and a swimming pool in the expansive grounds.
1–3 place Paul Boncour.
Tel: 02 54 32 32 01. www.
chateaudechissay.com

Chinon
Hostellerie Gargantua ££
This former palace with steepling towers, spiral stairs and wood and stone interior is now a charming hotel that has rooms at various rates to suit several budgets.
73 rue Voltaire.
Tel: 02 47 93 04 71.
www.hotel-gargantua.com
Hôtel Diderot ££
Within the old quarter and only a couple of hundred metres from the château stands this slickly run, pretty place, which has quirky, individual rooms and offers a homely welcome, with breakfast available on the shady terrace and supper indoors by a roaring fire.
4 rue de Buffon.
Tel: 02 47 93 18 87.
www.hoteldiderot.com

Loches
Hôtel de France ££
The budget accommodation in this well-presented, traditional tufa stone house is simple but homely, neat and scrupulously clean.
6 rue Picois.
Tel: 02 47 59 00 32. www.
hoteldefranceloches.com

EAST CENTRAL LOIRE
Orléans
Hôtel de l'Abeille ££
This old-fashioned building decked out with greenery and flowers overflowing from balcony boxes is very welcoming. Rooms are decorated in French country fabrics and patterned wallpapers, while the café-bar is atmospheric and inviting.
64 rue Alsace Lorraine.
Tel: 02 38 53 54 87.
www.hoteldelabeille.com
Jackôtel ££
A converted cloister with bare brick, beams and original fireplaces, this place is peaceful and popular for its reasonably priced rooms.
18 Cloître St-Aignan.

Accommodation

Tel: 02 38 54 48 48.
www.jackotel.com

Hotel d'Arc £££

This dramatic looking, centrally located hotel with an Art Nouveau façade has light, airy rooms with modern amenities and touches of individuality as well as elegant communal areas and a stylish restaurant.

37 rue de la République.
Tel: 02 38 53 10 94.
www.hoteldarc.fr

Blois

Anne de Bretagne £₤

Well-positioned on a shady square near to the château and the centre of town this good-value place to stay has basic but tasteful rooms and some secure parking. There is a sister establishment, Le Monarque, at the top of town offering reasonable rooms at similarly good rates.

31 av Jean Laigret.
Tel: 02 54 78 05 38.
http://
annedebretagne.free.fr/

Côté Loire £₤

This converted coaching inn is well placed on the bank of the Loire, with a number of cheerful rooms boasting river views. There is also a pleasant courtyard and well-regarded restaurant on site.

2 place de la Grève.
Tel: 02 54 78 07 86.
www.coteloire.com

Chambord

Hotel and Restaurant Grand Saint-Michel £₤

With unparalleled views of the château, guests at this country house have the grounds to themselves after closing. Rooms are tasteful and some overlook the château. There is a restaurant decorated with hunting trophies and terrace on site too.

place St-Louis.
Tel: 02 54 20 31 31.

www.saintmichel-chambord.com

Valençay

Le Relais du Moulin £₤

Next to a converted mill, this hotel has simple, purposeful rooms without fancy trimmings but at reasonable rates.

44 rue Nationale.
Tel: 02 54 00 38 00.
www.hotel-lerelaisdumoulin.com

THE EASTERN LOIRE
Sancerre

Les Logis du Grillon £₤

Charming bed and breakfast rooms or *gîtes* with plenty of character are available in this comfortable, quiet establishment, which serves up splendid breakfasts.

3–5 rue de du Chantre.
Tel: 02 48 78 09 45.

Enjoy stunning views over Chambord

Practical guide

Arriving

European Union (EU) residents visiting France need only a passport to enter the country. Citizens of the USA, Canada, New Zealand and most other western European nations need no visa unless they intend to stay for more than three months. Australian and South African visitors need a visa, irrespective of the length of their stay. If you hold a non-EU passport, check entry requirements with your nearest French consulate.

Travellers who require visas should obtain them in their country of residence, as it may prove difficult to obtain them elsewhere. Several types of visa are available – allow plenty of time to apply (two months is advisable).

By air

The region has three main airports with international connections: Angers, Nantes and Tours. Paris is also very convenient, especially if touring the eastern Loire.

By train

The Loire Valley is well served by the French rail system SNCF (Société Nationale des Chemins de Fer), with fast links to Paris. The *Thomas Cook European Timetable* (published monthly) gives up-to-date details of European rail services (and many shipping services) and will help you plan a rail journey to, from and around France.

The timetable is available in the UK from some railway stations and any branch of Thomas Cook, or by phoning *(01733) 416477* or you can buy online at *www.thomascookpublishing.com*.

In the US contact: Rail Europe for schedule, route and pass information. *Tel: (1) 877 257 2887. www.raileurope.com*

By ferry

There are numerous cross-Channel ferry services linking France to the UK: the nearest French ferry ports are St Malo (for the westernmost Loire Valley), Cherbourg, Ouistreham, Le Havre and Dieppe. These ports are served by Brittany Ferries, Condor and P&O. Irish Ferries have daily sailings in summer from Rosslare and Cork to Le Havre and Cherbourg.

By road

The *autoroutes* speed visitors through the Loire Valley, from Le Mans via Angers to Nantes (A11), from Paris to Orléans and Tours (A10), from Tours to Angers (A85) and from Orléans to Bourges (A71). The amount of toll payable depends on distance travelled.

Camping and caravanning

The region has many fine campsites, each graded by the tourist boards who rate the number of facilities on offer, from one- to four-star. The French love the great outdoors and almost every village has its camping site.

For more detailed information contact local tourist offices or: **Fédération Française de Camping et de Caravanning** (*78 rue de Rivoli, 75004 Paris; tel: 01 42 72 84 08*).

When travelling by road, vehicles towing caravans must keep at least 50m from other vehicles, have specially extended rear-view mirrors and be no more than 11m in length and 2.5m in width.

Children

Children are a natural and welcome part of any holiday in France. Most can sleep in their parent's bedroom for free or for a low supplementary charge. They are welcome in restaurants, many of which offer children's menus and high chairs. Only the grandest restaurants will turn a hair at the sight of a family invasion. When travelling by train, ask for discounts: children under four travel free; from four to twelve, they go at half price.

Climate

The nickname of the 'garden of France' is due to a combination of fertile soil and a mild climate. As soon as visitors driving south from the coast enter the Loire Valley, they notice a distinct lift in temperature. Frost and snow are rareties, but July and August can be quite humid, with temperatures in the high 20s. For most of the year, the pleasantly mild temperatures make this

an ideal area for touring and for holidays (as well as for growing grapes).

Conversion tables

Clothes, except for women's dresses, and shoes sizes follow the standard sizes for the rest of Europe. *See tables on p181.*

Crime

The Loire Valley is relatively crime-free, but never offer the temptation of visible valuables in the car. At the height of the season, handbags are always at risk in crowds. Report crimes to the local police – in big cities at the *commissariat de police*, in rural areas at the *gendarmerie nationale*. Take all your identity papers and, if relevant, vehicle papers with you. If your passport is lost or stolen, contact your consulate.

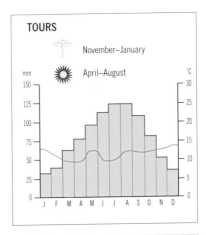

TOURS

November–January

April–August

WEATHER CONVERSION CHART

25.4mm = 1 inch

°F = 1.8 × °C + 32

Driving

Driving licences from all European Union member countries are valid in France, as are American, Canadian, Australian and New Zealand licences. Drivers should always carry the vehicle's registration documents and valid insurance papers. The so-called 'green card', the International Insurance Certificate, is also highly recommended, as is membership of a home-based breakdown/accident recovery scheme.

Road signs are international. Although *priorité à droite* (priority for cars approaching from the right) still applies in built-up areas, the rule no longer applies on roundabouts.

Dipped headlights should be used in poor visibility and at night. Right-hand-drive vehicles should have their headlights adjusted, or use patches to prevent dazzle, though yellow tinting is not required. Seat belts are compulsory, as are helmets for motorcyclists.

Car rental is easy in the region, with all the major international companies represented in the bigger towns; Citer is a reliable French company.

Speed limits

Urban areas: 50kph (31mph).
Single carriageway roads: 90kph (56mph). On wet roads 80kph (50mph).
Dual carriageway roads: 110kph (68mph). On wet roads 100kph (62mph).
Motorways: 130kph (81mph). On wet roads 110kph (68mph). Note that a minimum speed of 80kph (50mph) applies when overtaking in the middle lane.
Motorcycles of less than 80cc have a 75kph (47mph) speed limit.

Don't let the pretty countryside distract you on a winding road

Follow the signs

Road signs

Rappel is a reminder that speed limit restrictions continue.

Blue signs indicate motorways.

Green signs indicate main roads.

White signs indicate local roads.

Green signs with '*bis*' in yellow are alternative, quieter routes.

Yellow signs indicate a *déviation* (diversion).

Péage: toll; *Ralentir*: slow;

Sens unique: one-way street.

Electricity

220 volts 50-cycle AC is the national standard along with continental-style two-pin plugs. Adaptors are well worth buying before leaving home.

Embassies and consulates

Australia *4 rue Jean-Rey, Paris 75015. Tel: 01 40 59 33 00; www.austgov.fr*
Canada *35 avenue Montaigne, Paris 75008. Tel: 01 44 43 29 00; www.amb-canada.fr*

Practical guide

CONVERSION TABLE

FROM	TO	MULTIPLY BY
Inches	Centimetres	2.54
Feet	Metres	0.3048
Yards	Metres	0.9144
Miles	Kilometres	1.6090
Acres	Hectares	0.4047
Gallons	Litres	4.5460
Ounces	Grams	28.35
Pounds	Grams	453.6
Pounds	Kilograms	0.4536
Tons	Tonnes	1.0160

To convert back, for example from centimetres to inches, divide by the number in the third column.

MEN'S SUITS

UK	36	38	40	42	44	46	48
Rest of Europe	46	48	50	52	54	56	58
USA	36	38	40	42	44	46	48

DRESS SIZES

UK	8	10	12	14	16	18
France	36	38	40	42	44	46
Italy	38	40	42	44	46	48
Rest of Europe	34	36	38	40	42	44
USA	6	8	10	12	14	16

MEN'S SHIRTS

UK	14	14.5	15	15.5	16	16.5	17
Rest of Europe	36	37	38	39/40	41	42	43
USA	14	14.5	15	15.5	16	16.5	17

MEN'S SHOES

UK	7	7.5	8.5	9.5	10.5	11
Rest of Europe	41	42	43	44	45	46
USA	8	8.5	9.5	10.5	11.5	12

WOMEN'S SHOES

UK	4.5	5	5.5	6	6.5	7
Rest of Europe	38	38	39	39	40	41
USA	6	6.5	7	7.5	8	8.5

Ireland *4 rue Rude, Paris 75016.*
Tel: 01 44 17 67 00.
New Zealand *7ter, rue Léonard de*
Vinci, Paris 75016.
Tel: 01 45 01 43 43; www.nzembassy.com
UK *35 rue d'Anjou, Paris 75383.*
Tel: 01 44 51 31 00;
www.amb-grandebretagne.fr
USA *2 avenue Gabriel, Paris 75008.*
Tel: 01 43 12 22 22; www.amb-usa.fr

Emergency telephone numbers

Accidents (Police secour) *17.*
Ambulance SAMU *15.*
Breakdown it is well worth buying an
AA 5-Star insurance policy to cover any
serious breakdowns.
Chemist for emergency prescriptions,
contact the local police station.
Dentist for emergency dental care,
contact the local police station.
Directory enquiries *12.*
Doctor (SOS Médecins) Tours: *02 47
38 33 33;* Nantes: *02 40 50 30 30.*
European emergency number
112 (Free).
Fire (Sapeurs Pompiers) *18.*
Poisoning Angers: *02 41 48 21 21.*

Health and insurance

France has no mandatory vaccination
requirements, and no vaccination
recommendations other than to keep
tetanus and polio immunisation up to
date. Food and water are safe. As in every
other part of the world, AIDS is present.

All EU countries have reciprocal
arrangements for reclaiming the costs
of medical services. UK residents

should obtain form E111 from any post
office in the UK. This provides detailed
information on how to claim and what
is covered. Claiming is often a laborious
and long drawn-out process and you
are only covered for medical care, not
for emergency repatriation, holiday
cancellation and so on. You are
therefore strongly advised to take out a
travel insurance policy to cover all
eventualities. You can purchase such
insurance through the AA and most
travel agents.

Holidays

1 January New Year's Day
March/April Easter Monday
1 May Labour Day/May Day
8 May VE Victory in Europe Day
May (mid) Ascension Day
May (late) Whit Monday
14 July Bastille Day
15 August Assumption Day
1 November All Saints' Day
11 November Remembrance Day
(Armistice)
25 December Christmas Day

Lost property

Report to the local police.
For lost or stolen credit cards ring the
following numbers:
American Express *01 47 77 70 07.*
VISA *08 36 69 08 80.*

Media
Newspapers
Regional newspapers are more
influential than the national papers –

La Nouvelle République and *Ouest France* are on sale everywhere. English-language dailies are available in larger towns.

Radio
FM radio stations offer a choice of non-stop classical music (Radio Classique) or pop. France Inter (LW

1892) is the equivalent of BBC Radio 4, which can itself sometimes be picked up in the region.

Television
France has four state-owned TV channels and two private ones, but many hotels now have satellite TV with

ANNUAL MARKETS & FAIRS

Annual markets and fairs in the Loire Valley are a great occasion for local farmers and craftsmen to show off their wares and proudly display their local heritage.

JANUARY
Richelieu Foire des Rois (food and craft market).

FEBRUARY
Azay-le-Rideau Wine fair (last weekend).
Montlouis-sur-Loire Wine fair (third weekend).

MARCH
Angers Carnival.
Sancerre Old-fashioned market (Thursday before Palm Sunday).

APRIL
Amboise Easter wine fair.
Saumur Wine festival.

MAY
Angers Festival of the Quays (water sports).
Sancerre Cheese fair (1 May or next weekend); Wine fair (Pentecost weekend).
Orléans Fête de Jeanne d'Arc (first week).

Mennetou-sur-Cher Andouillette (sausage) fair (first weekend).

JUNE
Sainte-Maure-de-Touraine Cheese fair (first weekend).
Le Coudray-Macouard Village festival.

JULY
Amboise Hunting and fishing festival.
Tours St Anne's Day – garlic and basil fair (26 July).
Bourgueil Garlic fair (third Sunday).
Loches Evening street markets animated by theatre and music.
Sablé-sur-Sarthe Classical dance & music.
Saumur Carrousel (riding display).

AUGUST
Chinon Medieval market.
Montoire-sur-le-Loir Folk festival (second week).
Menetou-Salon Open wine cellars (third weekend).

Sablé-sur-Sarthe Classical music and dance festival.
Sancerre Wine fair (last Sunday).

SEPTEMBER
Amboise Melon fair (first Wednesday).
Bourgueil Wine fair (second Tuesday).
Montreuil-en-Touraine Bread festival.

OCTOBER
Menetou-Salon Wild mushroom fair (about 10 October).
Romorantin-Lanthenay Gastronomic fair (last weekend).
Sancerre Oyster fair (last Sunday).
Azay-le-Rideau Apple fair (last weekend).
Bourgueil Chestnut fair (last Tuesday).

DECEMBER
Saint Nicolas de Bourgueil St Nicolas fair.

Contemporary architecture marks the presence of business and industry

a huge range of European and American channels on offer.

Money matters

The euro, the single European currency, is operational in France. The euro has eight coin denominations: €2, €1, 50 cents, 20 cents, 10 cents, 5 cents, 2 cents and 1 cent; 100 cents make up 1 euro. Credit cards are accepted almost everywhere. In the major cities and towns, hotels, shops and restaurants often accept traveller's cheques in lieu of cash.

Museums

National museums are closed on Tuesdays. Students under 18 get in for free. Reduced-price entry is charged for 18- to 25-year-olds and the over-60s. Municipal museums are usually closed on Mondays. Most museums close for lunch, except in July and August.

Opening hours

Banks 8.30am–noon and 2–4pm weekdays; closed on either Saturday or Monday and at noon on the day before an official holiday.

Post offices 8am–7pm weekdays (until 5 or 6pm in smaller offices); 8am–noon Saturdays.

Food shops 7am–6.30 or 7.30pm; some open on Sunday mornings. Closed at lunchtime.

Practical guide

Other shops 9 or 10am–6.30 or 7.30pm; many are closed half or all day on Monday, and those in small towns and villages close from noon–2pm. **Hypermarkets** open until 9pm or later, Monday to Saturday (some do not open until 2pm on a Monday).

Tourist attractions opening hours:
There is a bewildering variety of opening hours between places to sightsee, museums, places of worship, shops, entertainment spots and banks. But in general all sights are open daily in July and August. Phone ahead when planning a specific outing.
Museums usually 10am–6pm; most are closed all/part of Monday/Tuesday.
Castles and abbeys open during daylight hours till 7pm summer/4pm in winter.

Churches 8am–noon and 2–7pm or later. Visits during services are discouraged.

Senior citizens
Produce a passport to take advantage of any discounts, irrespective of whether or not you are a French national.

Student accommodation
There are 16 Auberges de Jeunesse (youth hostels) in the Loire Valley region. Contact the French headquarters for information:
Fédération Unie des Auberges de Jeunesse (*9 rue Brantome 75003 Paris; tel: 01 48 04 70 30; www.fuaj.org or tel: (1) 44 89 87 27; www.hihotels.com*).

The local tourist office has up-to-date advice on what to see and do

Language

English is widely spoken in tourist areas, less so in the countryside. But whatever your location, you will find that your efforts to speak French, however limited, are appreciated.

yes	oui
no	non
please	s'il vous plaît
(any request or enquiry should be accompanied by this phrase)	
thank you	merci
good day/	bonjour
good morning	
(when addressing anyone in this way, it is common courtesy to add *monsieur* for a man, *madame* for a woman or *mademoiselle* for a girl or young woman)	
good evening	bonsoir
goodbye	au revoir
yesterday	hier
today	aujourd'hui
tomorrow	demain
the morning	le matin
afternoon	l'après-midi
the evening	le soir
man	un homme
woman	une femme
big	grand
small	petit
a lot	beaucoup
a little	un peu
open	ouvert
closed	fermé
hot	chaud
cold	froid
car	voiture
railway station	gare
bus station	gare routière
bakery	boulangerie
supermarket	supermarché
bank	banque
toilets	toilettes
post office	PTT, poste
stamps	timbres
chemist	pharmacie
hospital	hôpital

petrol	essence
airline	ligne à air
Do you speak English?	Parlez-vous anglais?
I do not understand	Je ne comprends pas
OK/agreed	D'accord
Where?	Où?
How much?/	Combien?
How many?	
Excuse me	Pardon
Have you a room?	Avez-vous une chambre?
Have you a room with a private bath?	Avez-vous une chambre avec bain?
How much does it cost?	Combien ça coûte?
I feel ill	Je suis malade
Have you a double room?	Avez-vous une chambre à deux lits?

0	zéro		22	vingt-deux
1	un, une		30	trente
2	deux		40	quarante
3	trois		50	cinquante
4	quatre		60	soixante
5	cinq		70	soixante-dix
6	six		80	quatre-vingts
7	sept		90	quatre-vingt-dix
8	huit		100	cent
9	neuf		200	deux cents
10	dix		300	trois cents
11	onze		1,000	mille
12	douze		2,000	deux mille
13	treize		1,000,000	un million
14	quatorze			
15	quinze		**Monday**	lundi
16	seize		**Tuesday**	mardi
17	dix-sept		**Wednesday**	mercredi
18	dix-huit		**Thursday**	jeudi
19	dix-neuf		**Friday**	vendredi
20	vingt		**Saturday**	samedi
21	vingt et un		**Sunday**	dimanche

PHRASES

How do you say…(in French)	Comment dites-vous…(en français)
Can you speak slower, please?	Parlez moins vite, s'il vous plaît.
Can you repeat please?	Pouvez-vous répéter, s'il vous plaît.
Help!	Au secours!
Wait!	Attendez!
Stop!	Arrêtez!
What's that?	Qu'est-ce que c'est?
Can I have…?	Je voudrais…?
This one/that one	celui-ci/celui-là
It's too expensive	c'est trop cher
I'm just looking	Je regarde seulement
What time do you open?	À quelle heure êtes-vous ouverts?
What time do you close?	À quelle heure êtes-vous fermés?
I would like to reserve…	Je voudrais réserver…
I have a reservation	J'ai fait une réservation
Single room	chambre pour une personne
Twin room	chambre à lits jumeaux
Double room	chambre pour deux persones/chambre double
With shower	avec douche
With bath	avec bain
Is there a good view?	Est-ce qu'il y a une vue?
Can I see the room?	Est-ce que je peux voir la chambre?
Can I have the key?	Est-ce que je peux avoir la clef?
Is breakfast included?	Est-ce que le petit-déjeuner est compris?
Bed and breakfast	chambres d'hôtes
Can we camp here?	On peut camper ici?
Tent pitch	un emplacement
Youth hostel	auberge de jeunesse
Which way is it to the…château?	Quelle est le chemin pour aller à/au…château?
Where is…?	Où est…?
Is it far?	C'est loin?
Left/right	à gauche/à droite
Straight on	tout droit
Here/there	ici/là
Close/far	près/loin
Corner	coin
Have you got a table?	Avez-vous une table libre?
I want to reserve a table	Je voudrais réserver une table
I am a vegetarian	Je suis végétarian
I'm having the €20 set menu	Je prendrai le menu à vingt euros
The bill please	L'addition s'il vous plaît

Telephones

Coin-operated phone booths are no longer common and the *télécarte* phone card has taken over. Buy one in a post office or *tabac* (tobacconists) to save time, trouble and money. The cards (50 units and 120 units) are much cheaper than a hotel call and simple to use.

Many phones now accept credit cards too. Cheap rates operate between 10.30pm and 8am and all day Sunday. French telephone numbers have ten digits, the first two indicate the region: the northwest, including the Loire, is *02*. When phoning France from abroad do not include the initial zero of the French number.

To make an international call from France, dial *00*, then the country code: **Australia** *61*, **Canada** *1*, **Ireland** *353*, **New Zealand** *64*, **UK** *44*, **USA** *1*.

For international directory enquiries dial *3212*.

Time

The Loire is one hour ahead of GMT in winter, two hours in summer. When it is noon in Nantes or Orléans, it is:
9pm in Canberra, Australia;
11am in Dublin, Ireland;
11am in London, UK;
6am in Ottawa, Canada;
6am in Washington DC, USA;
11pm in Wellington, New Zealand.

Tipping

Cafés and restaurants include all taxes and tips on their bills although people often leave their coin change as well.

After an extended stay at a hotel, it is customary to leave a tip for the chambermaid. Porters, museum guides, taxi drivers and cinema usherettes always welcome a *pourboire* (tip).

Toilets

There are public toilets in department stores, cafés and restaurants and there are self-cleaning *toilettes* (coin-operated booths) on the streets.

Tourist offices

For general information on the region contact:

Pays de la Loire CDT Pays de la Loire, *2 rue de la Loire, 44200 Nantes. Tel: 02 40 48 24 20; fax: 02 40 08 07 10.*
Centre-Val-de-Loire CDT Centre-Val-de-Loire, *37 ave de Paris, 45000 Orleans. Tel: 02 38 79 95 00; fax: 02 38 79 95 10.*

Travellers with disabilities

Access to the major tourist attractions is improving all the time. However, as most of the Loire's attractions are ancient castles and cathedrals, there are often real problems for wheelchair visitors. Although there are no overall guides for the region, the **Comité National Français de Liaison pour la Réadaption des Handicapés** (CNFLRH) does have leaflets (in French) on aspects of daily life in France.

The Ministry of Tourism (*www.tourism-handicaps.org*) also has relevant and useful information.

Index

Acknowledgements

Thomas Cook Publishing wishes to thank the AA PHOTO LIBRARY (RICK STRANGE), to whom the copyright belongs, for the photographs in this book (except for the following images):

DREAMSTIME 18, 71 (Richard Semik), 33 (Michal Sofron), 42 (Musat Christian), 61 (Lambert Parren), 125, 136 (Xedos4),
IMAGES-OF-FRANCE 10, 25, 39, 48, 114, 115, 139, 141, 154, 156, 162, 172, 173, 184
iSTOCK PHOTO 87, 88, 135 (Phooey), 119 (dbeghoura), 131 (jean-lucgc)
MARY EVANS PICTURE LIBRARY 64, 65, 97
ETHEL DAVIES 22, 58, 89, 93, 105, 108, 138, 180
PHOTOSHOT 40 (Hermann Wüstmann)
ALEX STEWART 4, 15, 50, 52, 91, 161, 177

The remaining pictures are held in the AA PHOTO LIBRARY and were taken by: ROB MOORE, with the exception of pages 43, 69, 84, 109, 111, 129, 151 which were taken by J EDMUNSON, pages 5, 27, 128 which were taken by BARRIE SMITH and page 80 taken by PAUL KENWARD.

For CAMBRIDGE PUBLISHING MANAGEMENT LTD:
Project editor: Jennifer Jahn
Typesetter: Donna Pedley
Proofreaders: Ceinwen Sinclair & Michele Greenbank
Indexer: Marie Lorimer

SEND YOUR THOUGHTS TO
BOOKS@THOMASCOOK.COM

We're committed to providing the very best up-to-date information in our travel guides and constantly strive to make them as useful as they can be. You can help us to improve future editions by letting us have your feedback. If you've made a wonderful discovery on your travels that we don't already feature, if you'd like to inform us about recent changes to anything that we do include, or if you simply want to let us know your thoughts about this guidebook and how we can make it even better – we'd love to hear from you.

Send us ideas, discoveries and recommendations today and then look out for your valuable input in the next edition of this title.

Emails to the above address, or letters to the traveller guides Series Editor, Thomas Cook Publishing, PO Box 227, Coningsby Road, Peterborough PE3 8SB, UK.

Please don't forget to let us know which title your feedback refers to!